Wed cont. again to ▮▮▮▮ ▮▮▮▮
beautiful sight ever ▮ **W9-BFS-843**
we set up camp on the river edge by
the waterfalls. What a honeymoon.
I supposed to have enjoyed more

Use Your Head in Tennis

at age 20. But then what fun is it
without arthritic spasms of the
hip sockets. Wild flowers not to
be believed. Mountain violets dasies
which are white & lavender black eyed
susans with yellow center. Took.
We are sleeping on the downslope of
the tent as last nite in the double down
was like a hoop da snort.
Thur. Good Chuck awakend at 7:30
& fished the great forks catching a
healthy rainbow returning to figure
breakfast Sausage oatmeal Breakfast
Bars are great. Ed went fishing
below the great fall of water were
two big Trout wholes did she not
catch to date the biggest of about
14"—2 lbs.. Then a short trek around
Ins moss lk. What a sight. (over)

made friends with a Buckskin trail horse from Maroon lake Campsite, one Appy looked for the world like Ziggy. We both took a swallow Pete dog & without saying with all of this magnificence we were a little homesick for the moment. We packed up after a yuk! lunch of horrible hamburger oh yes Charlie Tuna caught one more rainbow. Down the mountain I come with the patience of Job following it seems 3 mi a day is the extent of my trec up or down. Bad feet forced a stop. Charlie left to find a campsite. He was gone quite awhile when I realized a thunder storm was upon us I loaded my Jack 1st time by myself & hoofed it to meet Charlie. We ponchoed & made it to our little honeymoon cottage by the river below the beaver ponds. Home sweet home. Dinner of soup & steak (good) Then early to bed nice rain sleep & late to rise 8:30 — XXX

Bed Freed back to bed by a
rain storm — Not bad little siesta.
Brush cook by my lord & master

Use Your Head
in Tennis
Revised Edition

Bob Harman, with

Keith Monroe

at 10:30. Then off to the beaver pond
for Charlie while Tillie took tempduty.
More rain threatening + 4 hrs.
to go. Poor feet as the typical last
min. dash occurs.... I was right
on both counts the rain + Charlie's last
min dash. The long tree down in pour-
ing rain lightening and thunder became a mountain song. We stopped in
some pines + Charlie dropped a line in

KENNIKAT PRESS
PORT WASHINGTON, N.Y.
I couldn't do any
and hung another fish.
thing right. Snagged on rocks + branches
oh yes Charlie Tuna returned at 12:30
with 2 more Rainbow beauties one about 13"
Cont. Back page

Manufactured in the United States of America

Kennikat Press, Port Washington, N.Y., is the exclusive publisher of the paperback edition by arrangement with T. Y. Crowell Co.

1 2 3 4 5 6 7 8 9 10

Library of Congress Cataloging in Publication Data

Harman, Bob, date.
   Use your head in tennis.

   1. Tennis—Psychological aspects. I. Monroe, Keith. II. Title.
GV1002.9.P75H37 1974   796.34′2′01   74-10715
ISBN 0-8046-9111-8

Foreword by Jack Kramer

A lot of people were surprised when I began taking daily tennis lessons immediately after I came home from winning the All-England championship at Wimbledon and the U.S. championship at Forest Hills. But there was a very good reason why I did so: there is a tennis coach in Los Angeles who can help anybody to play better—including world champions.

That coach is Bob Harman. He is the man who has given postgraduate lessons, as you might call them, to many of the greatest champions in the game. Stars such as Bobby Riggs, Louise Brough, Margaret Osborne DuPont, Gertrude Moran, Lee Van Keuren, Allan Cleveland, and others have worked out with Bob Harman many times.

Bob is an exponent of what we call sophisticated tennis. He knows all the angles—the fine points—the subtleties that enable a smart player to beat a dumb one, even when the dumb player happens to be able to run faster and hit harder.

That's one of the reasons he's such a successful coach for all kinds of people. He takes middle-aged men and women and shows them how to beat younger players. He takes busy executives and shows them how to make the most of what scanty time they have for practice. He takes children and turns them into champions. He takes tired-out or elderly players and shows them how to play good, satisfying tennis without exhausting themselves.

He is a great analyst of form. He knows precisely how every stroke should be made, and why. Furthermore, he knows what flaws to expect. Because he gives lessons all day, every day, he can tell you what the common mistakes are, what to beware of in your own shotmaking.

That's the beauty of this book. There is nothing theoretical in it. Everything has been tested and proved, over and over again, in his own coaching. Bob Harman's book is ideal for any public-parks or club player who wants to improve. Even the careerists who play tournaments all year round can pick up some new and valuable ideas from it. I recommend it enthusiastically.

Contents

Illustrations

Use Your Head in Tennis

1 / Why This Book Was Written

Well, I'm back. It's been a long time.

In the twenty-four years since this book was first published, the game of tennis has changed drastically. It has evolved from a minor sport enjoyed mainly by socialites into a game that is currently played by more than ten and a half million people—young and old, professional and nonprofessional.

A Different Kind of Tennis Book

When I wrote the first edition, I decided even then that I was going to write a book that *everyone* would be able to read and understand. Most of my friends said that it was different. They said it helped them a lot.

Most of these friends weren't big-time tournament stars. They were just weekend tennis players of both sexes—the kind of people for whom I'd written the book.

I knew that tennis books were usually written with the aim of helping readers win the Wightman Cup or the Davis Cup. The authors assumed that their market was made up of redhot tournament hopefuls who practiced daily, who understood fundamentals thoroughly, who were strong and fast enough to hit like Helen Wills or Bill Tilden, and who wanted to be told how to become another Wills or Tilden. In other words, tennis books were for advanced, dedicated players.

That was fine. But how about the amateur who can play only once or twice a week? I had thought. Nobody seems to have much advice for him or her.

Cannonball serves and bullet volleys were worthy objectives for a few hundred young athletes who could spend hours and years perfecting them. But wasn't it also worthwhile to help the thousands of people whose strokes were strictly half-strength?

I knew that tennis wasn't exclusively a high society pastime. There were swarms of people at public courts and in tennis clubs who had very little leisure time, who never hoped to win a tournament. All they wanted was to have fun, and beat their own friends. Why not a book for these people?

Well, I wrote it. And it dropped dead—I thought.

Tennis, Everyone?

Meanwhile people's attitudes were changing. Tennis was losing its snobbery but not its status. As more and more people went on a health kick and looked for enjoyable ways of keeping fit, tennis turned into a growth industry. One old-line racket manufacturer increased sales by 44 percent in one year.

Housewives got slimmer because of brisk sessions on the courts. Mothers led their children to tennis classes almost as soon as they could toddle. Families planned vacations around resorts that featured tennis. John Gardiner, who started the country's first tennis ranch in California in 1957, pointed out, "People are finding they can have fun even if they are hackers."

All of a sudden, *Use Your Head in Tennis* came into its own. A British edition was published, then imported into the United States. A softcover edition was published, and sales took off. Tennis aficionados called it a "classic," and it became what people in the book trade call an "underground best seller."

It had taken awhile for the game to catch up with the book, but by 1974 enough changes had occurred so that the book had to catch up with the game. For one thing, I wanted to revise what I'd written about women's tennis. Women players have changed dramatically in two decades. Nowadays they aren't so willing to assume that men are better players than they are. Women of all ages are more athletic than they used to be. And the feminine invasion of tennis has been the biggest change in the sport; I've seen statistics indicating that four of every five new tennis players in 1973 were women. For every six adult men who play tennis there are now five adult women players, according to the President's Council on Physical Fitness and Sports.

Certainly the rise of attractive new stars such as Billie Jean King, Chris Evert, Julie Anthony, Evonne Goolagong, Marita Redondo, Peggy Michel, and others brightened up the game and increased public interest. Today there are often bigger galleries watching the women's matches than the men's. That seldom happened in the old days.

Therefore an up-to-date book for tennis players ought to be addressed equally to men and women. I've added a whole new chapter on women's singles and doubles, and revised the old chapter on mixed doubles. Beyond that, virtually every sentence in this book will apply equally to males and females. For the sake of brevity I'll usually just say "he" or "his" but I hope you'll consider these pronouns as shorthand for "he or she" and "hers or his."

Women have helped prove that two-handed strokes are more useful for the average player than I once thought possible, so I've included more advice on them. Types of equipment, styles of dress, and a few points of etiquette have changed with the decades, necessitating revisions in the text.

The tennis of the 1970s is played on a wider variety of surfaces than in the past, ranging from Sportface carpet to artificially slowed concrete. City landscapes are speckled with bubbles housing indoor tennis centers; right now there are at least 800 of these, lighted for day-and-night play, with scores more on the drawing boards. So I've inserted more information on how to adjust your play to different environments.

We never used to hear much, if anything, about tennis elbow or tennis toe or tennis leg. But with millions more players there are bound to be many sore anatomies. So I've included the best medical advice I can find.

Hackers Can Improve

There are plenty of things a mediocre player of either sex can do to acquire better strokes and make better moves around the court. I'm going to show you how to spot your own mistakes, and get rid of them. I won't tell you how to win championships, but I'll tell you how to acquire smooth, easy strokes that will stand up well in your own league.

Coaching an inexpert player is vastly different from coaching a star. I've done both for most of my life. I've seen all the errors that ordinary amateurs keep making over and over, and I've learned how they can eliminate those errors from their games.

There are many simple principles that tournament players follow almost unconsciously. These automatic adjustments are taken for granted by tennis writers—most of whom are tournament champs themselves, not teachers—and consequently seldom get into the books. I'm putting all those ABC's on paper.

There are plenty of more subtle methods that will enable one hacker to beat another. You'll find them in this book. For example, you'll find a new chapter on a training technique I recently invented, called "ghost doubles," that should make a much better doubles player of you. And you'll find another wholly new chapter on the major problem of returning hard-to-handle serves—a subject that I didn't think to cover when I wrote this book the first time.

There are ways of saving your legs, of compensating for short wind and sore arms and slow reflexes. Once you understand, you can use your head to save your strength. This book, if you use it right, will add many minutes to the time you can keep playing without tiring. And it will add years to your life as a tennis player.

How to Use This Book

I suggest that you go through this book once at a gallop, just hurrying along without stopping to study anything. Skim through it in one evening, if you can. That way you'll get the broad outlines of tennis theory in your mind. And you'll also have a better idea of where to find the answers to whatever perplexing problems pop up as your game develops.

Then start on a slow second reading, one chapter at a time. You needn't necessarily read the chapters in the order they appear. Study Chapters 2 and 3 first because they give you the basis of all sound strokes and court strategy. After that, pick out whichever chapters seem to apply most to you.

If you're bothered by your backhand, tear into Chapter 7 and let your serve and forehand wait till later. If you play mostly doubles, skip the chapters on singles. You ought to go back and master them eventually because they contain pointers that will help you in doubles, but Chapters 10–16 are full of information you can apply in every minute of doubles.

Don't try to follow all my advice at once. Don't even take one chapter and try to put it all into practice tomorrow morning. Instead, fix two or three ideas firmly in your mind, and bear down on those hard while you're playing. Keep concentrating on them until they become habits. Then pick out a few more ideas and build them into your game the same way.

When you're reading the chapters on stroke technique, take a racket in your hand. Practice in front of a mirror. Do *not* practice by hitting a ball against a wall, unless you want to practice rapid-fire volleying.

One of the essentials of correct stroking is to have a long follow-through. You just can't follow through smoothly if you're hitting against a wall because the ball is starting back to you while you're still finishing the stroke. You're bound to cut your stroke short and snap the racket into position to hit the ball again. If you don't, it goes by you. That's why practice on a wall is bad for your shots. The ball comes back too soon. You jerk and poke and hurry every stroke. (For a green beginner, who hasn't yet learned to meet the ball squarely, practice against a wall is good preliminary training. For anyone else, no.)

If you and a tennis-playing friend can read this book together, and practice together after each chapter, you'll both get a lot of extra value from it. When you read the chapter on forehands, go out and rally for an afternoon, constantly feeding the ball to each other's forehands. When you read about volleys, take turns at the net. Just work on one stroke at a time, and you'll be surprised how fast you take the kinks out of it.

Have Fun!

Let's not be grim about this. While you're on the tennis court, you should be enjoying life. Evidently you take tennis seriously or you wouldn't be reading this book. But I trust you'll never take it so seriously that you work yourself into a foaming frenzy over it. When a stroke goes haywire, laugh it off. When you lose a set, forget it.

This business of hounding a white ball over a net is taken up by different people for different reasons. Some reasons are good, some not so good.

If you take up the game to make new friends, that's good. Tennis is one of the classic social mixers. It's a polite, friendly game. Play it joyously—and considerately—and you'll make plenty of friends. Some people lose friends on a tennis court simply by playing as if lives were at stake. If you want to be popular, you'll always keep tennis a game, not a fight.

If you take up the game to lose weight, that's a mistake. This is probably bad for my business, but I must tell you that tennis is not an effective way to reduce. Even the fanatics who bounce around a tennis court for three or four hours in a broiling sun, wearing heavy sweat shirts, don't lose much weight permanently. They may walk off the courts pounds lighter, but they're so dehydrated that they drink a gallon of water. And the exercise gives them an appetite like an anaconda—so by the time they've finished dinner they're just as heavy as they were before.

Over a period of years tennis will convert blubber into muscle, perhaps, but it won't change your weight noticeably. If you're looking for quick changes, look elsewhere. Most of the coaches and doctors I know say that if you want to become your former self, the best way to do it is to eat less food.

On the other hand, if you took up tennis for the sake of your general health, that's good. It will tone you up—make you sleep better and eat better and feel friskier during the day. That is, provided that you keep it a game, play for fun, and knock off for the day when it ceases to be fun. Don't make work out of it. Don't play so long and hard that you can barely drag yourself home to bed afterward.

Winning or losing isn't the important thing. It's the social companionship that's important, and the exercise, and the mental cleansing that comes from completely forgetting everything else for a couple of hours while you concentrate on swinging a racket.

However, I'll admit that there's more satisfaction in winning than in losing. Everybody likes to look smooth on a court. And you can. No matter what your age, you can play gracefully, powerfully—and victoriously, if you learn the lessons in this book.

A smooth tennis game will help you earn a reputation for muscular control and nice judgment. But the odd thing is, you can play a smooth tennis game without being notably gifted with either of these qualities.

You have to be gifted, born with certain rare talents, to be a big tournament star. But to win consistently in club tennis, all you need is an understanding of certain exact principles, and a moderate amount of practice along the right lines.

Learning to play good tennis is pretty much the same proposition as learning to typewrite, or to bake cakes. Anyone can do it, if he's given the right instructions and follows them. Some people will become faster typists or better bakers than others, but nobody will fail to achieve adequate skill unless he's subnormal. That's the way it is with tennis.

Strategy is better than strength on a tennis court. An intelligent old man can beat a dumb young one. Just being able to hit hard and run fast isn't any great asset in tennis. A weaker hitter and slower runner can still win out, if he knows where to place the ball and how to anticipate his opponent's moves and how to make the most of his own stroking equipment.

The one greatest secret of success in tennis is to relax. Whaling the ball with all your might isn't the way to win. Gritting your teeth, clenching your fists, and cussing yourself out don't help. A calm player almost always beats an angry one. A flowing, effortless stroke is better than a quick, savage one. That's why I've told you several times already, and will keep reminding you all the way through this book, that you must play tennis for fun. When you stop having fun, you'll probably stop winning. Keep a song in your heart, and you'll be all right. I hope you'll study this book seriously, but I hope you'll have a good time with it. Let's go!

2 / The Secret of Ball Control

Don't Be a Murderer

There's at least one in every tennis club: the slam-bang, neck-or-nothing player who hits every ball as if he wants to batter it to smithereens. He never can understand why he has such difficulty persuading anybody, of high or low estate on the tennis ladder, to step onto a court with him. Even the club's topflight players make excuses when he suggests a game.

It can't be the way he plays tennis, he says to himself. Isn't his game as spectacular as anyone's? Doesn't he hit drives that are veritable bullets? There must be something else wrong. He wonders if he has galloping halitosis, or if club members think he beats his wife.

What he may never know—unless he reads this book—is that people dislike playing with him for the simple reason that he hits the ball too hard.

Does that make tennis players sound like sissies? It shouldn't. What a tennis player wants is a duel of drive and counterdrive—a chance to hit some balls and keep on hitting them—some running and some manuevering. What he gets against a slugger is a lot of work picking up balls.

Sluggers are the pariahs of the tennis courts because they hit virtually nothing except aces and errors. Mostly errors. There are no rallies. You hit one ball to a slugger, and then you walk into position to start the next point, because he's either socked it into the net or backstop, or else he's murdered it with an untouchable placement.

His placements, when he makes them, look impressive, but actually they're sheer luck. He never knows where the ball is going. He habitually sacrifices control for speed—and nobody enjoys playing with a man who lacks control.

Such a speed demon is not a good player. He hits harder than he really good players do. Even the great international stars don't try to pulverize the ball, except on service and an occasional overhead smash. Oh, their drives are faster than a club player's but not as much faster as you might think. The acoustics of a tennis stadium make each impact of racket against ball sound like a gunshot, and spectators at the big tournaments assume that the drives must therefore be red hot—but if you were playing against a tournament star you'd be surprised to find that his drives don't travel as fast as those of your club pest.

Tournament players know that it's useless to wallop a drive with their full strength because they can't control its flight if they do. About the only great champion who persistently tore the cover off the ball was Ellsworth Vines. Vines is the only tennis champion who became an outstanding golf professional. He now is the golf pro at the famous La Quinta Hotel near Palm Springs, where President Eisenhower had his home. His drives flickered across the court like summer lightning, clearing the net by perhaps half an inch and hitting no more than six inches inside the baseline. Vines is the only man in the modern history of the game who could murder the ball and still put it where he wanted it. When he was right, he could have crucified most of the legendary champions of other years. But he had to practice relentlessly to keep himself at the very peak of his game because his strokes gave him such a tiny margin for error that he could be beaten badly if his form got even a trifle ragged. In one big match he went down something like 6-0, 6-1, 6-0 against Bitsy Grant, the dinker par excellence whose greatest assets were steadiness and the ability to keep getting the ball back. Just like the slugger in your own club, Vines was either very good or very bad, the main difference being that Vines was usually the former and your acquaintance is usually the latter.

Easy Does It

Although the man who murders every ball is an annoyance or a joke to other players around his club, he differs only in degree from most of his clubmates. They don't realize it, but nearly all of them make the same mistake he does, to a less glaring degree. They hit too hard.

Ask any club pro, or any school coach, and he'll tell you the same thing: the besetting fault of the average player is hitting too hard. Nearly all once-a-week tennis enthusiasts try to use a racket as a battering ram instead of a precision instrument.

How about you?

Haven't you found that you frequently beat yourself through failure to control the course of your shots? Are you driving ball after ball a foot or two into foul territory? Are you smacking one into the back fence, or the next court, or the bottom of the net every now and then?

If so, the reason is almost certainly that you're hitting too violently to be accurate. You sometimes take such a ferocious whack that you hurry your swing, jerk at the ball, ruin your follow-through, and make a wild shot that depends entirely on blind luck to put it inside or out.

To cure all this, the prescription is simple:

Relax. Take it easy. Forget about trying to hit aces.

The way to beat your friends—and the way to enjoy tennis—is to hit a medium-paced ball, with control. If you'll slow down your drive a bit, take a full backswing, and a full follow-through, you'll find yourself placing the ball where you want it.

You'll also find yourself having more fun. The boys who go into tantrums and apoplexy on a tennis court, who throw rackets over the fence, who spend half their time hating the game and their partners and themselves are the boys who murder the ball and therefore fail to control it. How much happier they'd be if only they would settle for a smooth, graceful, accurate drive with moderate power! Then they would know where the ball was going when they hit it; they wouldn't be cursing and praying as they watched its flight. They could relax and think ahead to the next move by the opposition. They'd make far fewer errors and therefore wouldn't lose their temper. The whole atmosphere on the court would change, and everyone would enjoy the game more.

In all sports, easy does it. The boxer who takes a terrific roundhouse swing, and grunts with the effort of his punch, isn't the one who knocks out opponents. He can't aim his blows, and when they do land he hasn't got his weight behind them. A straight puncher like Joe Louis, who looks smooth and graceful even when he's knocking a man silly, is ten times as deadly as a wild, berserk swinger. Jack Dempsey could put a fighter to sleep with a hook that traveled no more than six inches.

Louis and Dempsey and all the other killers of the ring put their legs, hips, and shoulders into their punches, not just their arms. The big-league baseball pitchers throw with their whole body. The homerun hitters use an easy, flowing swing that produces power not by the speed with which they move the bat, nor by great effort of their arm muscles, but by the weight of their body behind the bat. Golfers who drive a ball a mile never hurry their swing. Whether it's a soccer ball, a hockey puck, a discus, or a tennis ball that you're propelling, the secret of power lies in a fluid, graceful, not-too-fast motion that gets your weight into it.

Just remember that fundamental principle, and you'll probably hit the tennis ball much better. If you've been playing tennis for ten years or more, you're not likely to make many revolutionary changes in your stroke techniques. Therefore this book will show you how to take what you have and build on it, how to smooth out your present strokes through minor changes rather than try to develop brand-new championship form. But these detailed mechanics come later. We'll tackle them in subsequent chapters. Right now, you should begin sharpening your game by making one simple resolution: resolve to slow down your strokes and not to try to murder any more drives.

The Sin of Wrist-Flicking

When you try to murder a drive, you probably draw the racket around behind your shoulder, flick it across your body in a sort of roundhouse hook with a vicious twist of your wrist, and end the swing with the racket coming to rest somewhere behind your left armpit. It's a stroke that is seen on tennis courts every day. That wrist-flicking drive looks spectacular because it really makes a ball smoke. Even if the shot lands far outside, as it usually does, the spectators' eyes pop—and maybe the opponent's eyes pop too—because the shot obviously took physical strength, and obviously traveled with murderous speed.

Yet it's a bad shot. You practically never see it in big-time tennis. It demands too much effort of the wrist and forearm, and, more important, it's a jerking, flicking shot which can't be controlled. You can't aim anything when you flick it. The only way to aim anything, when you're throwing or hitting it, is to move your hand in the same straight line that you want the object to follow.

So you'd better forget about that spectacular wrist-flicking drive. Forget about hitting with a roundhouse swing, and think about driving with a smooth, straight motion in which your racket follows through along the same line that you intend the ball to go.

Surprisingly, the average wrist-flicker doesn't need to make any drastic change in his stroking technique in order to get rid of his fault. He need only keep two thoughts in his mind:

1. Before hitting the ball, remember to hit it more slowly than usual.

2. During and after the hit, remember to follow through.

Follow-through is vital. And don't forget that it must be a follow-through in the direction of the ball's flight, not a follow-through toward the sideline.

Try it. You'll be amazed to find that you've stopped flicking your wrist, stopped jerking, stopped hooking. Just by stroking slowly and following through you'll straighten out your swing and control the placement of your shots. Your shots won't travel as fast as they did when you flicked your wrist, but they'll travel fast enough, and they'll land inside the court instead of outside.

Your greatest temptation to use this wrist-flicking shot will come when you're at the net and your opponent sends across a floater. The ball looks as big and soft as a balloon and you mentally smack your lips as you prepare to plaster it. So you flick your wrist and hit with all your might, and what happens? You belt it into the top of the net, or barely outside the line.

Club players miss these easy kills again and again. They hurry the shot, try to hit it too hard, and feel like biting a piece out of someone's leg when they miss. Even the professionals succumb to temptation on these easy kills sometimes. A few days before writing this chapter I was playing Jack Kramer, and in one of his rare mistakes he gave me a sitter in the forecourt. I had all the time in the world. I could have placed the ball anywhere I liked. But I wanted to make dead sure that Jack wouldn't get to the ball, so I flailed it with all my strength—and knocked it into the alley. I felt like breaking my racket across my knee.

We all have to keep a tight grip on our rash impulses when we get a chance for a kill at the net. We have to keep reminding ourselves, whenever such a shot comes up, to take our time, aim the shot, and slow down enough to make it good. Steel yourself to do this, and you'll spend much less time in that special little hell occupied by tennis players when they miss easy shots.

"Feel" the Ball

Maybe you're not sure, when you hit your drives, whether you're stroking well. You can't see yourself, and perhaps there's no expert on hand to watch your form and criticize it. So, even though you're struggling to get rid of that wrist-flicking style of stroke, you're not sure whether you have succeeded.

There's one easy way to check up on yourself. You can tell whether your stroke is good or bad just by the feel of the ball against your racket—and therein lies the big secret of stroking smoothly and controlling your shots. Feel the ball!

When you follow through properly, with your racket moving in the same direction as the ball, the ball will naturally be flattened out against your racket for an instant longer than it would be otherwise. Therefore you'll feel a heavy, solid, soul-satisfying thwack of the ball against gut while you're hitting it.

It's that longer contact between ball and racket that gives accuracy. Conversely, it's the instantaneous glancing contact of racket moving in a different line from ball that sends the ball flying off at unpredictable tangents whenever you hit it with that murderous flick of your wrist.

In every good stroke—whether it's a drive, a volley, a lob, or a smash—the racket must meet the ball squarely and solidly. Whenever it does, you'll get an unmistakable feel of solidity against the racket, of gut and ball in contact during an appreciable interval of space and time. You'll feel that good substantial thump all the way through your racket and up your arm.

Always stroke *through* the ball, and it will feel good against your racket. Furthermore, it will go where you want it. Just make your whole arm motion, from start to finish of the swing, follow the line you want the ball to travel. That's all you have to do. If your racket moves along that line, the ball will too, and you'll find yourself controlling your shots.

Constant attention to the feel of the ball, as your racket strikes it on every shot, will give you instant warning if your shots are getting sloppy. Among tournament players you'll often hear remarks like, "I lost my feel." What they mean is that they lost their follow-through, thereby losing the solid feel which they'd learned to expect in hitting the ball.

This feel is almost as important in volleying as it is in driving. A good volley should feel solid to you. If it doesn't, you're hurrying, jerking, and hitting the ball a glancing blow—most common fault of club players at the net—and, while it may travel with the speed of sound, its destination is unpredictable. Don't stroke a volley, just get your racket squarely into the path of the ball; then block it back, or "punch" it back if you want more speed. Get your shoulder and body into the hit, which will give you controlled power, and you'll feel that rich smack when you hit.

Some topflight players are said by their opponents to hit a very "heavy" ball. Maybe you've heard the expression. Don't let it confuse you. What it means is a ball that comes at you with more speed than you expect.

Don Budge always hit an extremely "heavy" backhand. When you played to his backhand, you'd see him take an apparently easy swing, and you'd think his drive would be a soft one. But as it crossed the net you'd realize it was faster than you thought. By this time you'd started your swing, and therefore Budge's ball nearly knocked your racket out of your hand when you hit it.

The reason a Budge backhand felt heavy was that opponents misjudged the speed with which it would travel. Don had a way of gliding forward and stepping into the ball which increased the speed of impact, even though his racket hardly seemed to swing at all. Similarly, Pancho Segura's two-handed stroke produced more power than it appeared to, and was forever surprising players by the speed at which it ricocheted off the ground. Consequently he had a reputation for hitting heavy balls. Kramer's forehand is a heavy one too because he's loose as ashes when he hits it, and his racket doesn't look as if it's moving quickly. His long arm gives him more leverage than you realize, and he pours the rest of his weight into the stroke with such superb smoothness that you think his effortless-looking drive will produce an average-speed ball. Among the newer stars, Stan

Smith probably hits the heaviest ball. He doesn't glide into it as Budge did, but he gets under it and makes it feel like a brick when it hits your racket. Chris Evert, a champion women's player, also hits a solid heavy ball. She hasn't much of a serve, and no net game, but opponents can't get to the net against her because her ground strokes are so jarring.

There are players who bang the ball hard yet aren't said to hit a heavy ball simply because they flail with such spectacular speed and violence that opponents realize the ball will come fast. John Newcombe is an example. He works terribly hard on the tennis court. He grunts audibly when he serves. His racket fairly screams as he whaps a drive; there's nothing gliding or effortless about him. Youth and strength have been his main assets.

Rosewall is another smoothie who probably will be around a long time. He makes the game look easy.

You may never become good enough to acquire a reputation for hitting heavy balls. Such deceptive smoothness usually takes years of daily polishing. But if you'll forget about bashing the stuffing out of a ball and work for easier strokes with the smooth follow-through that gives you a solid feel against your racket, then you'll be able to enjoy tennis for the rest of your life. You'll control your shots, you'll be relaxed and happy while you're playing, and you'll be a popular opponent in any tennis club you join.

3 / How to Anticipate

Wake Up!

Eddie Burns is sixty-five years old. But he can put up a good battle against players thirty years younger, and he can play all afternoon without dragging his feet. Why?

"He has a marvelous sense of anticipation," according to the gang at the club here in Los Angeles. "He never runs, but he always seems to be in the right place at the right time. He starts after the ball much sooner than most of us."

It's true that Eddie has a far better sense of anticipation than most club players—but there's nothing marvelous about anticipation. It's simply a matter of keeping alert, of using your eyes, and of thinking—which most players don't, but which Eddie does.

Unfortunately there is a widespread notion at tennis clubs that anticipation is a mysterious inborn gift, like the ability to multiply six-digit figures in your head; or else a supremely difficult skill that can be mastered only by years of daily practice. All expert players have it, but practically all once-a-week players lack it, which has strengthened the superstition that it's devilishly hard to acquire.

Yet Eddie, and others like him I could name, are the living proof that it's possible to cover court efficiently without being either highly trained or talented or even fleet of foot. Let's analyze how they do it.

First of all, they *start moving instantly after hitting the ball.* That's a simple thing, yet how few players do it!

Consider yourself. When you hit a shot from near the sideline, do you wait a fraction of a second to see where it lands? You shouldn't. You should be moving toward the center of the baseline as soon as the ball leaves your racket. Never delay in getting away from that sideline. If you do, a moment later you'll probably be sprinting hard to retrieve a shot on the other side.

In fact, it's a sound rule *always* to ease over toward the center, even if you're only a step or two away from it, the instant you've hit the ball. (Assuming, of course, that you're in the backcourt, and playing singles. In forecourt your position should be somewhat different, and obviously doubles is another game entirely. We'll get to that later.)

When you wallop a hard drive that may nick your opponent's line, do you stand there craning your neck—and maybe putting some body English on the ball, or praying, or swearing—until you see whether it goes in or out? That's a common habit, but a bad one. Wake up! Get moving! Assume that your drive will be in, and start walking into position for the return. You can be pretty sure that your opponent's return will be shallower than usual, if yours has hit near the baseline. Therefore you ought to be ambling forward while your own shot is still in the air.

If you want to take the net, keep moving steadily forward from the moment you hit. Don't stop to watch where your shot lands. It still makes me grit my teeth, even though I see it happen at the club every day, when somebody smacks a hard drive, stops, and *then* gallops in. If you stop when you hit, you'll usually be late getting to the net. Wake up! Get off the dime! If you're thinking about what you're doing, you can tell as soon as the drive leaves your racket whether it's going to be deep enough for you to come in behind it.

Once you do take the net, it's more important than ever to stay awake. If your opponent lobs, why stand gawking for a full second, waiting to see how high it's going? Start easing back before he hits the ball. As soon as he lowers his racket head in that telltale low backswing, you can see that he's going to lob. Bobby Riggs is almost the only player alive who can disguise a lob. So wake up, and back up! You needn't be afraid of retreating too far. Just keep your eye on the ball, and as it soars upward you'll be able to judge approximately how deep it will land. If you see it's shallow, you'll have plenty of time to step forward again and put it away. On the other hand, if it dusts the baseline, you still won't have to rush to get it on the bounce.

When you're volleying at the net, it's vitally important to slide into position for the next shot as soon as you've volleyed. Once again, don't wait to watch where your shot bounces. Get ready at once for your opponent's return. However, you should station yourself differently, now that you're in the forecourt.

Instead of waiting at the center of the net, you'd better move well over to one side or the other, depending on the direction of the volley you've just hit. If you volleyed to your opponent's forehand, edge over to your own left. If your volley went to the other sideline (his backhand), you'll do just the reverse: you'll drift over into your own forehand court.

You'll see the reason for this when you look at Figures 1 and 2. The section between the broken lines shows the area within which your opponent can return the ball.

See how little angle there is for him to cross-court?

If he tries to pass you by aiming across the part of the net you've left unguarded, his shot will hit the net, or land outside the court. So your strategy is to station yourself in the center of that small area within which he can return your shot. This means, clearly, that you'll move several feet away from the centerline after volleying toward the sideline. In the rare cases when you volley to the center, you'd obviously better get to the center of the net immediately.

One more point about anticipation while you're at the net: Get on your toes! Too many a player stands flat-footed while his opponent is starting his swing. He should get up on the balls of his feet as soon as the ball sails into enemy territory.

Even a topnotch player, if he's tired or loafing, is sometimes passed at the net by a shot that's only three feet from him. Why? Because he's not on his toes! I mean that literally. Physically. Don't put your heels on the ground, except during a lull. When your opponent is hitting the ball, bend a little at your hips and knees. Lean forward onto the balls of your feet. You'll be surprised what a difference it makes. You'll find yourself making a faster start to cut off any passing shot the opposition attempts.

Use Your Eyes

Another great secret of anticipation is to *keep your eye on the ball.* If

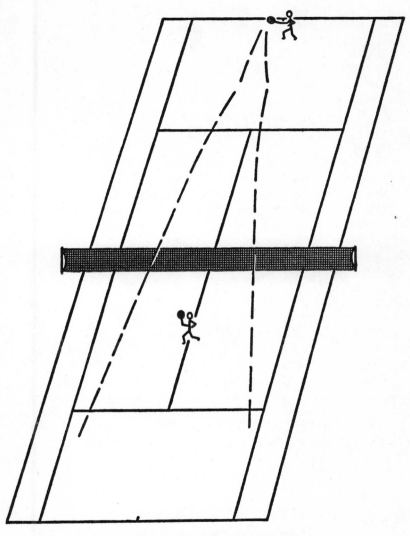

Figure 1. When ball is hit to the center of court,
net player takes position at center of court.

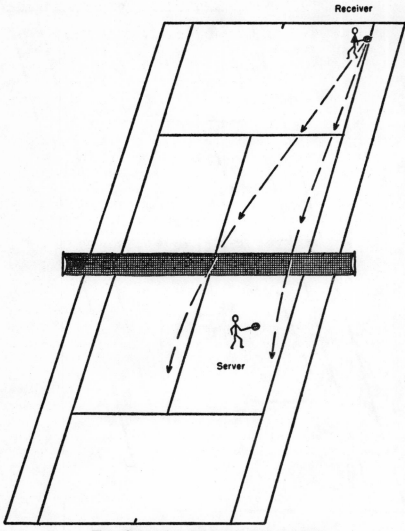

Figure 2. Net player places himself in the center
of the area where the opponent can return the ball.

you're looking at it the instant it leaves your opponent's racket, you see immediately where it's going, and how fast.

Sports fans often speak in wonderment of the fielder who starts for a baseball "with the crack of the bat," or the hockey goalie who lunges across the net to stop a shot at the same instant that it leaves an opponent's stick. Their secret is the same as the tennis expert's: they keep their eye on the ball. In tennis, try to remember always to watch that ball as it comes off your opponent's racket—as it approaches—as you hit—as it goes back toward him.

You may think you always watch the ball, but probably you don't. Most Sunday players unconsciously take their eyes off it even while they serve. Even champs let their eyes wander occasionally. They look at the ball as they hit, but they forget to keep looking while the other player hits. That's one reason a star sometimes makes a string of poor shots. When he realizes what's wrong, and reminds himself to keep watching the ball, his accuracy and anticipation come back to par.

You can hit the fastest drives that come at you if only you watch them from the instant they start. There is no such thing as "blinding speed" on a court if your eye is on the ball. You've plenty of time, even against a champion's drive.

Now we come to a more mystic principle of anticipation, one that's something of a trade secret, known to full-time players but not to club players. Yet it's a simple secret that any dub can readily teach himself to use, if he will.

In brief, the principle is to *watch your opponent*, as well as the ball, while he's hitting the ball. Difficult? Not so very. Player and ball are together during the stroke. You can train yourself to watch the whole picture. And it's important that you should.

Every player gives away the direction of his shot during his backswing. Even among the great champions, the give-aways are obvious, but the champs' shots are generally so good that you can't do much about it even though you know what's coming. Among club players, however, the give-aways are downright unmistakable, and there's plenty you can do about it!

Begin by watching your opponent's shoulders and upper arms for a few games. See what he does with them as he starts the shot, and then where the ball goes. Next time he hits, ask yourself if he's doing the same things with his shoulders. If he does, you'll notice the ball goes in the same direction as previously. If he doesn't you'll find it traveling in a different direction, or with a different depth and pace.

Probably he swings his left shoulder much farther around before hitting a forehand cross-court. Or drops his left shoulder and raises his right one before driving down the line. If his elbow is in as he hits, the ball is likely to go straight, or to his right; if his elbow is out, he's likely to drive to his left. On his backhand, you'll probably see his right shoulder going farther back as he starts to hit diagonally than it does when he hits straight.

Now watch his racket a while. Where does it go on the backswing? He'll undoubtedly raise it much higher in preparation for one kind of shot than for another. Also he'll swing it far behind him for a straight shot, perhaps, and wide outward for a cross-court.

How about his hips? They twist much more if the ball is going in one direction than another. How about his left arm (if he's right-handed, or his right arm if he's a left-hander)? You'll find it's a regular semaphore, signaling in advance the kind of shot he's going to make. How about his knees? Probably he bends them, or hitches one up, in preparation for some pet stroke. How about his feet? Doesn't he slide one forward, or draw it back, as a tip-off to various shots? Everybody does. And all these unconscious warnings are especially noticeable among club players, most of whom have rather eccentric ways of stroking which you can soon come to recognize. Just use your eyes, and think about what you're seeing.

As a matter of fact, you ought to be using your eyes for this same purpose when you're just a spectator, if you're watching someone you expect to play eventually. Always look to see what he does before hitting the ball, and then what kind of ball he hits. Learn to associate before-and-after, cause-and-effect, backswing-and-result. The give-aways are different with every player, but if you develop the habit of watching for them, you'll soon be noticing them without thinking, and heading automatically in the right direction before the ball even starts toward you.

Use Your Head

Now for your postgraduate lesson in anticipation. When you've overcome your bad habits of standing still after a stroke and forgetting to watch the ball, when you've learned to look at player as well as ball and remember what you see—then you're ready to learn the higher anticipation that comes from headwork.

Ever watch the manager on the bench at a big-league baseball game? Then you've seen him wave to an outfielder, motioning him toward a different spot. And perhaps, after the fielder has moved, you've seen the batter hit directly to him.

Even if you haven't noticed the manager signaling, you've certainly seen infielders and outfielders shift position a step or two when a batter comes to the plate; and you've seen the ball batted straight at one of them. It happens every inning. That's anticipation, in baseball. The same seemingly miraculous foresight is just as possible in tennis.

Fielders know where to stand for a batter because they know, from past observations, where he usually knocks a certain type of pitch. Catchers and pitchers know what pitches to give him because they know—also from past experience—which ones he has most trouble hitting. Big-leaguers keep indexes on every player in every club in the league: what balls he likes and dislikes, where he hits high inside throws and low outcurves and all the rest. Day after day they watch, remember, check their data, change it if an opponent's habits change, add new notes as they discover additional weaknesses.

You should do the same in tennis. Tournament players do. You can too, with less brain strain than remembering the fall of the cards in bridge or the best routes to take in driving to various friends' homes.

The best place to begin mastering this knack is on the sidelines. Instead of idly watching the flight of the ball, ask yourself questions as you watch your friends play.

Look at Joe Bleaux. Here comes a ball to his forehand corner. What will he do with it? Down the line, or cross-court? Will he get much depth? . . . Hmm. He overdrove the baseline. And the ball landed outside the sideline, too. Maybe he doesn't like them in his forehand corner. Let's see what happens the next few times he takes one there.

Assuming that Joe is an average club player, he'll almost always hit approximately to the same spot from that forehand corner of his. He won't cross-court half the time and put it down the line or into the center the rest of the time. After you've seen him hit long diagonal drives three or four times from that spot, you can be sure he'll do it nine times out of ten. And you'll know, the instant you've hit wide and deep to his forehand, that you'd better move back to your right for his return.

Furthermore, you can be pretty sure what will happen when you storm the net and put a ball into his forehand corner. His return will be shoulder-high, to your right, where you'll easily murder it. Against Joe, then, your net position will be farther to the right than it normally would be after volleying to that forehand corner. (However, this is all preliminary speculating, after seeing him return a few drives. Don't be too sure of it until you've checked to see whether he handles a volley differently from a drive when it's in that corner. And check it again when you've abandoned your spectator position and started playing against him yourself. Because of differences in your speed and pace, your drives and volleys may react a little differently against his racket than someone else's did.)

Here comes a shallow ball to Joe's backhand. Where does his return go? Does he hit it high or low? Fast or slow? To right or left? How does his stroke differ, when he's running for a ball, from when he's standing waiting for it?

Here's one down his backhand line. How does he like it? Where does he put it? Here's another to his backhand, but it's coming at him cross-court this time. Handles it differently than he did the straight one to the same spot, doesn't he?

Keep on watching him. Every time he makes an error, remember what kind of shot he was trying. Club players miss the same shot again and again for twenty years. If you want to beat your opponent, observe what shot he always flubs.

What does he do at the net? Is his forehand volley better than his backhand? Does he always volley down the line on his forehand?

Watch him when he's returning service. What does he do with a low ball on his backhand? You can bet it will be the same thing, virtually every time. Learn what it is, then put your serve there and stroll into position for his return. Keep on mentally cataloguing his responses to various kinds of serves. You'll notice some that he always handles well, others he always handles weakly.

At a big tennis tournament, the best competitors spend lots of time scouting each other. They're not lolling at the refreshment tables when there's a match involving someone they fear. They may have seen him play many times before, but they still want to look for clues that will help them anticipate his shots when they go up against him. Maybe he's corrected a weakness that used to bother him. Maybe he's slowed down, or speeded up, in returning various shots. Maybe he's hitting deeper or shorter, lately, than he used to from certain positions.

One reason tournament entrants from southern California win so frequently in all parts of the world is that the headquarters of the Southern California Tennis Association maintains up-to-date card files on all the best players from every other locality. When a southern Californian returned from a trip, he reported to the late Perry Jones, the master-mind of the S.C.T.A., with data on the reactions of every outlander he's opposed. The data is pooled so that any southern Californian can have it when he tackles that particular player. Every New Englander and Southerner and Briton and Australian is certain to find his weaknesses being pounded relentlessly from the first game to the last, whenever anyone from the S.C.T.A. machine is confronting him. The seemingly magical anticipation shown by top-flight Californians never fails to astound the galleries. Thorough briefing before a match is what gives them that anticipation.

This sort of scouting will be easier for you, if you're a casual player, than it is for the full-time tennis careerists. The chances are you play most of your tennis with a handful of friends, meeting them over and over again, instead of battling your way through tournament fields of forty or fifty strangers. Your friends' reactions on a tennis court are vastly more predictable than the tournament shark's reactions. In match play a man doesn't repeat the same shot under the same circumstances with such consistency as you'll find in club play; tournament players deliberately mix up their shots and keep trying new maneuvers.

Furthermore, your friends' errors are likely to be much more glaring than a specialist's are. The Wimbledon and Forest Hills crowd have to look for two or three tiny flaws in one another; you can find a half dozen gaping holes in every one of your acquaintances.

It may not be easy to find all these holes the first time you try. Remember that this is an advanced and sophisticated skill toward which you're now working. Start by concentrating on just one of your friends, and only when you're watching him from the sidelines. In the beginning you'll find it hard to observe and remember very much while you're actually playing against him. Just watch for one trait at a time, while you're learning. Get his backhand figured out before you start to keep tabs on his forehand. Gradually you'll build up a rough working knowledge of four or five things he does constantly.

Then, when you take the court against him, you'll soon find it easy to apply this knowledge. You can go on to spot his other weaknesses and strengths as you test his reaction to your own shots. By this time you'll have formed the habit of asking yourself questions, and remembering the answers, whenever you watch anyone play. It won't be too long before this sort of headwork comes naturally to you on the court as well as in the grandstand. Almost as automatically as you make the left and right turns on your way to work each day, you'll start to right or left or forward or back while your opponent is still getting ready to hit the ball. You'll find yourself drifting to the right place in plenty of time without having to run. And spectators will say, "Gee, what marvelous anticipation!"

4 / Let Your Forehand Flow

Smooth Out Your Stroke

Maybe you've been playing tennis for years. Or maybe you play just once or twice a week, with little time for practice. In such cases, it's silly to try to rebuild your strokes. I wouldn't advise you to try it if I were coaching you personally, and I don't advise you to try it while studying this book.

Instead of rebuilding your game, you should keep the strokes you have and concentrate on smoothing them out. Only in rare cases, when a player has such a radically wrong stroke that he gives himself a sore arm by using it, should he try to break himself of his habits and start all over to learn a brand-new way of hitting the ball. It's easy for a youngster to change his stroke completely; his muscles aren't set, his habits aren't deeply ingrained, and he can mold himself in entirely different habit patterns within a few practice sessions. Also, an older player who is willing and able to practice daily for an hour or so can eventually revise his game. But, for the rest of tennis-playing America—for the many thousands of men and women, boys and girls who merely want to play well enough to beat their own friends and have fun while they're doing it—a brand-new stroke isn't the answer. The answer is sandpaper on the present stroke. Smooth it out. Polish it up. Make minor changes and additions. Presently that awkward old stroke will become a serviceable weapon.

I've coached countless dubs who have developed into sound, steady players simply by smoothing out the strokes they'd already acquired. Those strokes were faulty, and never would have worked in tournament tennis. So what? These players weren't interested in winning Wimbledon or Forest Hills. They just wanted to enjoy a good game of tennis on Saturdays and Sundays. So we took those wrong strokes, let them stay wrong, and just put a longer follow-through on them, slowed down a quick, jerky movement into a rhythmic flowing one, maybe eased out a crooked elbow or a stiff knee action. We didn't try to transform the grip. We didn't try to change the angle at which racket met ball. We didn't even try to eliminate bad habits of footwork, if they were so ingrown as to be reflexes. We simply added a few new habits to the old ones, thereby compensating for them.

You can do the same for yourself. Without abandoning your old stroke, without trying to break yourself of habits that are so strong you're a slave to them without ever being conscious of them, you can teach yourself to stroke smoothly.

Let's begin with your forehand. That's where I always begin in coaching a new pupil. The forehand is the stroke you can use in rallying back and forth, so you can practice it a lot. Then we'll take up your serve, in the next chapter. With a decent forehand and a decent serve, you can play a respectable game of tennis even if your backhand is horrible. We'll get to the backhand in Chapter 7 and tackle the more specialized strokes later in the book.

Don't Lose Your Grip

First, a few words about the way you grip your racket. The chances are, if you've taught yourself, that your grip is incorrect. Never mind. If it feels good to you, don't try to get rid of it (unless, as I said before, you're young, or you're willing to practice a great deal). You can still give a good account of yourself, even holding the racket wrong. But you ought to analyze the way you do hold it, so you can compensate for whatever mistake you're making.

There are three different forehand grips: the western, the eastern, and the continental.

The western grip is passé now. You practically never see it in a tournament any more. It was the grip used by the old-time California champions—Morrie McLoughlin, Billy Johnston, and the like. For the record, here's how it goes:

Lay your racket on a bench or table. The racket head is now parallel to the ground, of course. You reach for the handle and grasp it in the natural way with the palm of your hand perpendicular to the ground and with your thumb to the left and your fingers twining around it so the handle settles comfortably in your palm. Okay. You are now holding your racket with the western grip. (See Figure 3.)

Figure 3. The western grip.

For the eastern grip, you give the racket handle a quarter turn in your hand, so that the head is perpendicular to the ground, instead of parallel as it is in the western grip.

Is that clear? In case it isn't, here's another way of describing the eastern grip. Reach out, empty-handed, as if you were going to shake hands with someone. Fingers pointing ahead, thumb on top and pointing upward, palm of your hand at right angles to the ground. Now, with your left hand, take your tennis racket and hold it with the head of the racket parallel to the palm of your hand. There you are. Slide the handle into your hand, and you're holding it with the eastern grip. (See Figure 4.)

I happen to be a westerner myself, but I use an eastern grip. So do Arthur Ashe, Stan Smith, Rod Laver, Roy Emerson, Cliff Richey, and practically all other competitive players in America today. It's the grip that gives you maximum power and maximum safety with minimum muscular strain.

The continental grip, with which Fred Perry won a world's championship, was a holdover from his days as a table tennis champion. In this grip the racket head is moved an eighth turn clockwise from the eastern grip. In other words, when you're holding the racket in the eastern grip—as if the top edge of the racket head were pointing to the figure twelve on a clock face—just shift your grip by turning the racket head until that top edge points midway between the numbers one and two on the clock. Now you've got the handle in the continental grip (Figure 5).

Some brilliant European players have used this continental grip. René Lacoste, the great French player of the twenties and now more famous for his "alligator" emblem line of tennis clothes, and Ilie Nastase, with their lightning reflexes, basing their game on speedy retrieving rather than power, were well suited to it. The continental grip doesn't give you any power, but it's a good grip for scooping a low ball off the grass. In Europe of the 1920's, when all big-time tennis was played on grass or clay and there were no sluggers, this way of holding a racket was fashionable. But nobody could use it unless he had lots of leisure for practice because it pays off only when you have delicate touch and timing.

As you'll find out if you experiment with the continental grip, you have to roll your racket head around the ball at just the right instant—or else you bloop the ball into the bleachers. You have much thinner margin for error than you do with the eastern or western grips. You need perfect coordination when you twist your wrist, arm, and shoulder to bring that racket head around the ball during the moment of contact. It's a good grip if you don't hit hard, and if you want to spend years perfecting your stroke. Otherwise, no.

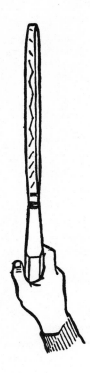

Figure 4. The eastern grip.   Figure 5. The continental grip.

The western grip was popular a generation ago because it was used by the tennis giants of those days. They picked it up more or less by chance in teaching themselves the game. Sluggers such as Maurice McLoughlin, the California Comet, who invented the American twist service, found that when they held the racket this way they could hit like houses falling down and get a lot of spin on the ball, making it drop faster. However, the muscular effort involved in driving with the western grip meant that nobody could use it unless he had the physique of Paul Bunyan.

The western grip went out with button shoes because the scientists and experimenters of the game proved that the eastern technique was sounder and easier. You can get just as much zing into a drive, holding your racket with the eastern grip, and not work half as hard at it. Furthermore, when you're playing on grass you'll kill yourself trying to use the western because it's almost impossible to hit a low ball that way—and balls take a low bounce on grass, of course.

The last big star who tried the western grip was Don Budge, the first player to win the grand slam, the four big national championships. He learned his tennis with that grip. But when he buckled down to make himself a champion, he switched to eastern. Like all the other full-time tennis players of the modern era, he learned that the eastern means more accuracy and less effort. You see, there's practically no way to mistime a ball when you hit it with the eastern grip because your racket head meets it squarely and you're stroking through the ball. But there are a million ways to mistime it when you use the continental or the western because your racket isn't moving through the same path as the ball is. That's why the eastern gives you more control.

If you're a self-taught player, you're quite likely to use a grip that's midway between the western and eastern. That is, when you "shake hands" with the racket, the top edge of the racket head is pointing to ten or eleven on a clock face—instead of to nine, as it would in the western grip, or to twelve, as in the eastern.

Such a grip is the natural one for many people. It's not good enough for tournament tennis, but it's good enough for matches around the public parks or the tennis for fun. The drawings are for your guidance if you have big-time tournament ambitions, or if you're young enough to change easily.

Analyze Yourself

Let's go on to study your forehand as it is. What mistakes are you making, and what can you do about them?

I'm assuming that you've read Chapter 2 carefully and have taken it to heart. This means that you are convinced in your own mind that you follow through smoothly, that you hit easily instead of hard, and that you "feel" the ball when you drive.

There shouldn't be any question about that last point. Either you feel it or you don't. I mean really feel it, with a rich, solid thud along your hand and forearm, which can happen only when the ball flattens itself out against your racket for an appreciable instant.

As to the first two points, however, you could be fooling yourself. Let's find out.

We'll look at your follow-through first. Hit a forehand drive, and then freeze motionless when you finish your follow-through. Now take a look at your racket. Just where is it? And at what angle?

The racket head should be at a right angle to the ground. Perpendicular to the ground, in other words—like a coin standing on edge. It should *not* be parallel to the ground. Is yours?

Furthermore, your racket should be reaching as far ahead—toward the net—as possible. This means to the full length of your right arm. Don't let your follow-through finish with the racket somewhere around under your left armpit, or behind your right ear, as all too many players do. If your right elbow is bent, your follow-through is bound to be wrong and your racket will end in the wrong position, which you'll notice as soon as you check up on yourself.

The orthodox way of planting your feet for a forehand drive is to point your toes toward the sideline with your left hip toward the net, and place your feet along the imaginary line you want the ball to travel. Let's assume that you've lined up your feet this way. Now, when you finish your follow-through, your racket should be just an inch or two to the left of that imaginary line on which both your feet are planted. Your whole right arm and shoulder should be pointing along that line.

Try it out in front of a mirror. You'll immediately discover that you need a loose swing of your hips and shoulders in order to finish in the position I've described. Your shoulders must move through a half circle. Your hips must be flexible and turn with your shoulders. Your right elbow, while not stiff, should be as nearly straight as it is when you relax your arm completely.

Now, the odd thing about this position is that, if you finish in it, all the earlier parts of your drive will have been fairly smooth and flowing. By following through correctly, you unconsciously correct many mistakes. You avoid the common fault of pulling up with racket, shoulders, and knees while hitting the ball—because whenever you pull up, your follow-through ends with the racket coming to rest in the vicinity of your right shoulder or ear. (I'm assuming, throughout this book, that you're right-handed. If you're not, simply read "right" for "left" and vice versa wherever they appear.)

Another fault of thousands of unskilled players is that they use too much wrist and arm, too little shoulders and hips, when they hit a forehand drive. You've seen that sort of drive on every club court. The arm is drawn back, then swishes forward across the body as racket meets ball. The torso is practically motionless. Hips don't turn. Shoulders stay where they are from beginning to end of stroke. Everything is done with the arm—and with the wrist, which turns the racket in the act of hitting the ball. Very bad!

The kind of forehand drive I've just described is the "flick" drive about which I already made some unkind remarks in Chapter 2. The follow-through, after such a wrist-flicking swat, brings the racket head to a halt parallel with the ground and in the general neighborhood of your left elbow. Generally, your right elbow is sharply bent in this follow-through.

If you're one of the unfortunate addicts of this flick, straighten it out by thinking about your shoulders and hips. Get them turning. Make yourself pivot on your hips as you hit the drive. Put your shoulders into it, with an easy flowing turn that brings your right arm (fully extended, remember?) into line with the flight of the ball away from you as you finish your follow-through.

From now on, keep checking up on yourself. Take a look at the position you're in as you finish following through each forehand. If that position is right, your whole drive can't help being approximately right.

That flowing motion, with a long, easy follow-through, will give you a streamlined forehand drive even if you're not gripping the racket quite right. If you happen to use the old western grip, when you hit a forehand drive you'll get best results by slowing down your stroke. Try to "feel" the ball as much as possible—which will mean that you won't roll the racket face around the ball quite so much when you hit it.

If, like most of the once-a-week players, you use a maverick grip about halfway between the western and eastern, you can compensate for this awkwardness by, again, working for a long, smooth, graceful stroke with plenty of follow-through. Feel that ball. Hit through it. The basic principles of smooth stroking are the same no matter what your grip.

Once you get so you're turning your hips and shoulders, and following through nicely, you won't have to bother too much about footwork. Too many people think, when they miss a shot, there must have been something wrong with their footwork. That's baloney. The hips are more important than the feet. Oh, I know that most textbooks tell you never, never point your toes toward the net while hitting a forehand drive. But Jack Kramer faces the net when he hits his forehand. You can too, if you understand the principle involved.

In his backswing as he prepares to hit the ball, Kramer twists his hips and his whole upper body so that his left side is turned toward the net. Then his hips rotate through a half circle, and at the end of the follow-through his right hip and right shoulder and right arm are all pointing to the net. Even though he places his feet differently, his upper body goes through the same motion as any other correct player's does. He's in exactly the same position, from the belt up, as is a player who hits a good forehand with toes pointing to the sideline.

Therefore, if you're chained to an iron-bound habit of pointing your toes to the net as you hit, don't worry about it. Let your feet stay that way. Just give some attention to your upper body. Make sure that it turns to face your right sideline before you drive, then pivots on your hips to face the left sideline as you follow through.

You ought to practice this kind of drive anyhow, even if it's not your usual custom to point your feet toward the net. There are plenty of times, in returning a fast serve, when you won't have time to shift your feet and point them toward the sideline. Work on your hip pivot so you can stroke from either angle and still finish your follow-through with your upper body in the same position, no matter where your feet are. Once you get this down pat, your forehand drive will be the same whether you're running or standing still, facing the net or the sideline. Regardless of what your feet and legs are doing, so long as you're in balance, your upper body can always turn through that smooth easy pivot from the hips.

You Jerk!

Now, if you've followed all instructions up to this point, you still may be making one serious mistake. In fact, I'd be willing to bet that you are. The odds are heavily in my favor: this is a mistake that the vast majority of all players—including good ones, whenever they forget themselves for a few minutes—keep on making unless it's called to their attention.

You can have a fairly smooth follow-through, and you can be feeling the ball as you stroke through it. Still you may not have the easy flowing stroke you should. You may—in fact, you almost certainly—jerk when you hit the ball.

Here's what I mean. From the instant your racket starts to move forward toward the ball until it finishes the follow-through it should be one continuous flowing motion, at the same speed from start to finish. No quickening or slowing at any point along the path of the racket.

Now, think about your own drive as you make it. Isn't there an acceleration of your racket at the instant you make contact with the ball? Aren't you swinging just a little harder at the mid-point of your stroke than you are during its beginning and end?

Experiment a little. Make your forehand drive through empty air, with no ball. Then hit your same forehand, with a ball. Notice a difference in the speed of the two swings? Notice a slight quickening just before your racket meets the ball? That's what I mean by jerking.

Jerking is an almost universal fault among fair-to-middling players. Even the topnotchers find themselves jerking a little, sometimes, when the pressure is on and their nerves are strung tight. The minute any player gets nervous and tries too hard, he begins jerking.

The trouble with a jerk is that it robs you of some of your control. When you jerk you make more errors. Therefore it's really important, once you've learned follow-through and feeling the ball, to keep watching this little matter of acceleration as you hit. Make your whole stroke a continuous flow at the same speed, as if the ball weren't there at all. Just forget about the ball; stroke through its path, and you'll meet it all right. This is the last secret of a successful forehand drive. It isn't hard to learn, even if you play only rarely, provided you keep thinking about it while you are playing. And what a difference there'll be in your game, once you do learn it! You'll make fewer errors. Better yet, your drive will be so effortless that you can keep hitting forehands all day long and never get tired. And your friends will remark, "Boy, that's a graceful forehand you've got now!"

5 / Service with a Smile

On tennis courts all over the country the whole summer long, suffering amateurs are losing points over and over again the same way. They hit their first serve with all their might—into the net; then they dish up a soft, fat second serve that anybody can handle with ease.

In other words, their first serve is much too hard, and their second serve much too easy. Probably you have that trouble yourself. Let's do something about it.

Let's work for a smooth effortless first serve that you can control. It won't be the cannonball that you're probably trying to hit now. But it will go in, more than half the time—which means that you can use practically the same serve, with slightly less speed, for your second serve too, and be sure of not double-faulting.

You'll be amazed what a difference there'll be in your whole game when you have a reliable first serve, even though it's just moderately paced. For one thing, you'll be able to use it to maneuver your opponent around. Your control will put the ball where he doesn't like it. You'll have him on the defensive immediately. You'll make him receive service farther back, instead of letting him take it closer to the net, as everyone does in preparing for the second serve.

For another thing, you'll save a lot of energy. Your first serve won't take as much out of you as it does now. Furthermore, you'll be serving only once instead of twice on most points. Those extra swats you avoid making, by getting your first serve in regularly, will be money in the bank when you're up against a tough opponent. You'll feel fresher in the late stages of the match—which is often the difference between winning and losing.

It's Smart to Slice

The serve I recommend for you is the overhead slice serve. Practically all the champs use it for the first serve, with varying degrees of spin. If you're smart, you won't try to hit it nearly as hard as they do—because you're probably not in the physical condition they are, and probably don't have the time for practice they do. A really hard serve demands more exertion than the average person can summon. Furthermore, the only way to put a hard serve into court regularly is to practice it for hours on end. A tournament player takes a boxful of balls onto a practice court and serves several hundred times in succession. After a few years of this, he has a serve that's both hard and accurate.

If you're not in the physical condition of a top athlete, with boundless endurance and razor-keen coordination, don't try to serve fireballs. It takes too much out of you. Instead, use the same serving technique that the big-timers use, but gentle it down a bit. Make it easy on yourself. Here's how.

For the overhead slice serve, take hold of your racket handle in the eastern grip I described in the previous chapter. Then turn the handle about a one-sixteenth turn clockwise. If the top edge of your racket head pointed to the numeral twelve on a clock face when you held the eastern grip, then that same edge should point midway between twelve and one for this slice service.

Stand with both feet planted firmly on the ground—left foot forward, of course, if you're right-handed. Your left shoulder should be pointing toward the court into which you will serve. To begin, let the weight of the racket pull your right arm down full length; then as your right hand starts smoothly up again in one continuous motion, your left hand starts upward too. That's important. Both arms should rise together.

From here on, the action of your right arm should be exactly the same as if you were throwing a baseball. Your arm goes back, comes up, then forward and down—following through with the typical throwing motion so that your hand crosses your body and finishes somewhere beside your left hip. That brings the racket head down near the ground, on the outer side of your left foot.

Every club player has his own style of serving, and usually it's a pretty eccentric style. No two are alike. Some players follow through on the wrong side, bringing the racket down past the right hip instead of the left—and wonder why their arm gets sore so often. Others don't follow through at all. Others throw the ball up too soon, or too late, or too short, or too high, or too far to the side. And so on, endlessly. That's why I can't write a prescription to cure everybody's ills at the baseline, unless I were prepared to make this book encyclopedia length.

But I can tell you how the serve should be hit—as I just have—and I can tell you some of the most common faults. That little matter of throwing the ball up is more important than you probably realize. The usual error is to flip it up with a wrist motion. That's bad because you can't always toss the ball where you want it, and it usually goes up too quickly so that you have to hit it jerkily before you're ready. The right way to throw the ball up is with a straight movement of the whole arm, not just the hand and wrist. Just let your left arm come up at the same time your right does, and place the ball up there above your head as your right hand is drawing back for that "throwing" motion. You should let go of the ball when your left hand is about even with the top of your head, and the ball should go about as high as you can reach with your racket. Get the feeling of placing the ball up there with your fingertips.

It's amazing how many fair-to-middling players forget to keep their eye on the ball as they serve. No wonder they can't serve accurately! It's a cardinal principle of baseball, golf, and every sport in which you swat an object with an implement, that you always—repeat, always—must look at what you're hitting. Think about this the next few times you're serving. Keep reminding yourself to watch that ball. Just this one simple little act may improve your serve surprisingly.

Another simple act which makes a big difference is follow-through. It's just as important in the serve as it is in the drives. I've seen countless dubs convert a feeble, erratic serve into a good, dependable one by nothing else than reminding themselves before each serve that they must follow through smoothly forward and down across their body.

Tenseness is another besetting sin at the baseline. How many players have you seen go bustling back to the line as if they had to catch a train, then rear back fiercely on the right foot, yank the racket down and up behind them like a tightening catapult, and finally flail the ball before their opponent is even ready? I see it happen every day on club courts. Nothing makes a receiver madder than to have his opponent serve before he's in position—but a sizable percentage of players do it, all absorbed in their own violent effort, never waiting or noticing anything except themselves.

Next time you're walking back to serve, take yourself in hand. Slow down. Breathe deeply. Loosen your muscles. Then plant your feet, look at them to make sure they're behind the line, look at your receiver to see whether he's set, and finally start serving—still with a relaxed flowing movement. Let your feet stay where they are until you've hit the ball; some tournament players go up on their toes, but that's an extra effort which takes its toll in a long match, and you can't afford it unless you're bursting with energy. If you want to follow through with your right foot after hitting the ball, you can, but it's better not to. Always try for the loose, easy movement of tossing a baseball, as if you were a pitcher warming up lazily a half-hour before game time. Easy does it. No grunts. No teeth-gritting.

As soon as you get the hang of this fluid motion with a sweeping follow-through—and you'll be startled how quickly you do get it, once you've begun putting your mind on it—you can speed it up a bit, and groove more of your weight into it. As long as your muscles aren't tense, you can serve that ball into court with respectable power. Furthermore, you can keep on doing it all day, and never get tired. It's a strong serve, but effortless. I've proved that to myself. I play tennis as long as ten hours a day—six days a week. And it's no strain because I've cultivated a smooth, easy stroke that takes nothing out of me.

Accuracy comes with practice. You'll probably never be a sensational sharpshooter, unless you make tennis your full-time occupation, but you can become accurate enough to plaster your pals. Some day when you have a spare half hour, go out alone on a tennis court with as many balls as you can round up. Just serve them over, slowly and easily, concentrating on putting them all into the backhand corner of your imaginary opponent's service court. Then walk to the other end of the court, collect all the balls, and serve them back—this time trying for the forehand corner of the court. Get in the habit of shooting always for one corner or the other—not the extreme corner, but a yard or two inside it. The point is to sharpen your marksmanship enough so that you never give the opposition a ball in the middle of the service court. Always pull him off to one side or the other—preferably his backhand side, since that's the weakness of most players. When you've fed him a few on the backhand, you'll probably notice him edging over more and more to that side, so he can take your serve on his forehand. That's the time to spot one in the forehand corner. He'll be enough out of position so that you can sometimes ace him without exerting yourself. At least you can force him into a weak and hurried return which will leave you in a commanding position.

Where to Stand

In singles, it's almost always sound practice to serve from within a foot of the center mark on the baseline. You may think you're being frightfully deceptive and tricky by altering your position, moving out toward the sideline to serve, but actually you aren't gaining anything. It's no easier to serve—and no harder for the receiver to return your serve—when you stand farther from the center. You're simply lengthening the distance between you and the point where the ball lands—which weakens rather than strengthens your attack. The tournament sharks have made tests and experiments for a half century and always come back to the conclusion that the center is the best place from which to serve.

You may have seen Okker, Laver, Dent, and Alexander, or one or two of the other top players vary the spot on the baseline from which they serve. Okker in particular moves clear over to his backhand sideline for an occasional serve. He does it because he has a deadly accurate serve with a sharp break, which can pull an opponent far out of position on the backhand side. The same is true of the few other international stars who try this strategy. They are so accurate, and have so much spin, that they can pull the receiver out of court. I don't recommend this for club players. Their serves aren't good enough. If they move to one side to serve, they leave half the court open and give their opponent a serve which he can usually return into unguarded territory for an ace.

Doubles play is something else again. Move about two-thirds of the way to the alley (that is, two-thirds of the way to the line which is the sideline

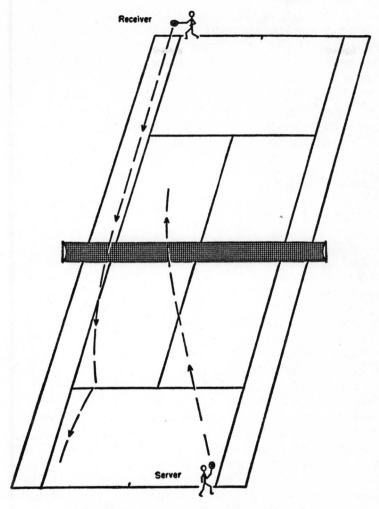

Figure 6. When server moves over to his own
alley and serves, receiver stands correspondingly
closer to his alley. (Notice how down-the-alley
shot would make server out of position.)

in singles) when you serve in doubles. The main reason for this is to station yourself in the center of whichever half of the court you'll be covering. Your partner, of course, covers the other half. He should be stationed close to the net, and as near to the center line as he can without leaving more than a foot or two of the alley uncovered.

Occasionally I meet someone who argues, "My serve always lands past the service line. If I stand a few feet behind the baseline to serve, I correct for that error and my serve goes in." Maybe so, but there's nothing shrewd about such strategy. You're simply handicapping yourself, and feeding your opponent an easier serve, in order to get it into court. You might as well serve on your knees, or dig yourself a hole at the baseline and serve from there. When you move back from the baseline, you're making yourself smaller in relation to the net. You're shortening the height from which your ball is hit, and lengthening the distance it has to travel, which gives your opponent more time to get ready for it. Tall people have an advantage in tennis. Never shorten yourself.

The way to stop hitting the ball too far, on service, is to change the angle of your racket head. Get the racket above your ball more as you hit. On the other hand, if you're hitting into the net most of the time, you're probably not throwing the ball quite high enough, or else you're hitting too late. Try to place the ball a little higher as your racket meets it.

That Feeble Second Serve

The second serve is the worst weakness of virtually all non-tournament players. Having missed their first serve, as they do three-fourths of the time, they're forced to resort to tapping the ball across in order to make absolutely sure that it goes in. They've never learned how to send over a safe, easy serve without making it a clay pigeon for the opposition.

Even in tournament tennis, the second serve is the acid test that shows up the difference between champions and also-rans. Nearly all competitive players have a good first serve. But only the headliners have a good second one. It's a key to their success.

Here's why that second ball is actually more important than the first. When a player gets into a tough match, if his second serve isn't strong and reliable, he'll be afraid of it. Getting his first serve in will seem all important. Consequently he'll be tense and overcautious and serve either a fault or a too-easy ball.

On the other hand, if he has a good second serve that he knows he can send over all day without missing, he'll be much more relaxed on his first serve. He can wallop it hard, without nervousness. He can even gamble on hitting it extra hard whenever he needs an ace.

The average player's game would be enormously improved just by the addition of that one weapon to his armory: a reasonably fast but foolproof second service. It would mean the difference between going on the defensive as soon as he serves the second ball—which is what happens now—and keeping the offensive—which is what he could do with a sound second serve.

If you cultivate this overhead slice serve I've been talking about, it's the answer to your second-ball problem as well as your first ball. Probably you're not enough of a gambler to hit your second serve as hard as your first. That's all right. Just use that slice on your second ball, but make it a slower and gentler swing than your first one, with a little more slice or a little more spin (of the kind we shall describe in the American twist serve) and it will practically always go in. It won't be an invitation to a massacre, either. It will sail fast enough so that your opponent will be kept away from the net, and it will have enough spin so it isn't likely to go dangerously near the line.

In doubles, your first serve should be almost as easy as your second serve is in singles. Remember that the object of every maneuver in doubles is to get to the net. If you put over a thunderbolt serve, it will come back before you have time to get into the forecourt. But a serve that takes more time to reach your opponents gives you more time to move forward. So that's the kind of serve you need.

The average player always serves too hard in doubles. If you've ever watched championship doubles, you've probably noticed how seldom anybody tries a fast serve. It simply isn't smart. The usual attack is to send over a medium-paced serve which clears the net by about three feet, drops inside with a good margin of safety, and bounces sharply off toward the side. While it's in the air, the server is coming in to join his partner at the net. The sidespin on the rebound pulls the receiver out of position and leaves an opening into which the men at the net can hammer a volley. Now, the best serve to get this result is the American twist. I'm not recommending it for anyone except muscular, well-trained athletes, but I'm including it for the sake of completeness.

How to Serve the American Twist

The key fact about this serve is that your racket face is moving upward and sideward as it meets the ball. This gives the ball a spin which makes it kick to your right on the bounce. Thus the receiver has to take it on his backhand. Worse yet for him, the ball has a high bounce. A high backhand is much harder to hit than a low backhand—in fact, for most players it's the hardest stroke in tennis.

The disadvantage, for you, is that the American twist takes lots of oomph. You really have to grunt when you serve this one. You must throw the ball above your left shoulder, then bend yourself back like an archer's bow, bend your right elbow sharply so that the racket is between your shoulder blades, and hit the ball a glancing blow while your racket is still traveling upward. The face of the racket moves across the ball from left to right.

Most championship players, masculine gender, use the twist service for their second ball. They like it because it moves across the net in a higher arc than the slice service, which means that it drops more steeply. Thus it's practically a lead-pipe cinch to land inside the service court. Once it lands, that sharp-breaking bounce to the receiver's left is going to pull him into the alley.

You seldom see a woman player, even a champion, serve a pronounced American twist. Helen Wills never did. It's too tiring. Most readers of this book probably aren't in as good condition as women tournament stars. Let them keep that fact in mind when they debate whether to take up the American twist.

Far better, most public-park and club players should concentrate on the slice serve and get it well enough so that they can use it with varying degrees of speed. They should save the full power for special situations, when the receiver is creeping up too close, for example, or when they're at a crucial point of the match and want to gamble. Their normal first serve, in singles, should be powerful but effortless, slightly below their full speed. First serve in doubles should be as well placed as they can possibly make it, with very little worrying about steam. The second serve, in either singles or doubles, is the gilt-edged security. There should be no gamble about it at all. You ought to be able to put it in play five times out of five, yet never give your receiver a cripple. With a smooth slice serve, you can do exactly this, just by slowing down from your normal first serve.

Shun the Freaks

There are quite a number of freak services. There's the reverse twist, hit with a sharp wrist twist from right to left; this gives the ball a high bounce to the left, but you haven't much control or accuracy. Another serve is the side spin, which Jack Kramer has made into a formidable weapon on his second serve. It's simply a more drastic version of the slice. For this one you hit the ball well out in front of you and bring the racket around it from left to right. In other words, you hold your racket more to the side, thus giving more slice to it. This gives it a low bounce and pulls it sharply to the receiver's backhand.

There have been sidearm and underhand serves in the early days of the game, and once in a great while you even see somebody who tries to whack the ball with a double-handed grip. Such novelties have never lasted. They're erratic and easy to return for point-winners once the opposition gets used to them. Practically nobody in tournament tennis tries freak deliveries. Any freak serve takes plenty of practice to acquire—and if the tournament players, who have all the time for practice that there is, don't think it worth while to put these serves in their bag of tricks, why should you waste time trying to master them? Get yourself a smooth, rhythmic slice service, and you'll be all right. You'll even get to the point where you can smile, instead of clenching your teeth, as you prepare for a serve that you're sure will be good!

6 / Many Happy Returns

The Second Most Important Shot

In the previous chapter we considered the most important shot in tennis, the serve. Practically everyone who spends much time at tennis develops an adequate serve—because of its obvious importance and because anyone can go off by himself with a pail of tennis balls and practice it intensively.

But the *second* most important shot, the return of service, is seldom played well. Nearly all run-of-the-club players are poor at it. And even in tournament play, statistics show that more errors occur on this particular shot than on any other.

Returning service is the second most important shot because we all are forced to attempt it on half the points we play. Yet I'm forever surprised at how few people are consistently good at it, and how little attention is given to it in instruction.

The average tennis player has learned a lot about returning service, in the same sense that an avalanche victim has learned a lot about snow. He's learned that strange afflictions strike him the moment he takes his stand behind the baseline. He often freezes into a wide, stiff-legged stance that makes him look like a flamingo with arthritis. And he jerks at the ball as if he's swatting a mosquito.

How often do you hear your friends wail, "My forehand and backhand are okay in rallies—so when I return a serve, why can't I hit it right?" How often do you yourself feel like a disaster area for the same reason? Yet it isn't difficult to return serves well, even when they come across with plenty of zing or a tricky spin. All you need is to make yourself remember a few basic rules.

Four Rules for Receiving

First of all, stand *several feet* behind the baseline when you await the first serve.

Too many otherwise smart players think they should crowd the line, as if they must hit the ball quickly before it bites them. This often means they must take the serve on the rise, which calls for real expertise. Worse yet, on the baseline they give up a precious split second in which to take a step and start a swing. And furthermore they lose the advantage of having a slower-moving ball to hit. No wonder their service returns go awry.

For the second serve, of course, you can move up to the baseline or inside it, if your opponent usually serves slower and softer for safety. However, while receiving either the first or second serve, there are other rules that apply.

The second rule concerns your bodily stance. You should be in a semi-crouch, both feet on a line parallel to the baseline. Your hips and knees should be bent and flexible. Your weight should be forward on your toes and the balls of your feet, with your heels barely touching the ground. Keep reminding yourself not to stand flatfooted, not to lock your knees.

The third rule concerns the position of your racket. Day after day I see players await service with their racket held across their body, its head somewhere around their elbow or shoulder.

Always keep your racket ready to start either a backhand or forehand return. This means holding it well out in front of you, pointing toward the net, racket face vertical. As you hold the racket, both your hands should be in line in front of you, almost as they would be if you were pulling yourself along a rope. Your left hand (assuming you're right-handed) is up near the throat of the racket, holding it lightly in position, while your right hand grips the handle as usual. Thus you have an equal distance to move your racket whether the serve comes to your left or your right.

The fourth rule is the most important. It's the simplest yet hardest to remember—the basic rule we advised you to follow continuously, in Chapter 3: Keep your eye on the ball!

A Key for All Sports

Watching the ball is the key to hitting well in tennis, just as it's the key to good hitting (and catching) in other sports. The commonest mistake of the average player is not looking directly at the ball as he makes contact with it.

For some reason it's harder to watch the ball when we return service than at any other time. Maybe the server's commotion distracts us. Or maybe we worry about him and try to see whether he's rushing the net or moving to one side or another. Forget him momentarily. If you watch the ball he's probably in your field of vision anyhow as his serve comes toward you.

Try to keep uppermost in your mind that you'll watch the ball as the server throws it up, as he hits it, as it approaches, and especially as you make your return, hitting through the ball with your wrist firmly locked and your hips turning. If you'll fix this habit firmly, you'll find yourself getting your racket into position for the stroke before the ball even crosses the net; taking that first step sooner; and consequently making smoother returns.

What Else You Can Do

Now for a few fine points that can add extra polish to your returns.

Just before the server tosses the ball up and you fix your eyes on it, watch his eyes. Most servers unconsciously dart a quick glance at the corner they intend to aim for.

Also take note of the server's racket as it makes contact with the ball you're watching. Does the racket go straight through the ball? If it does, then the ball's course will be straight all the way.

Or does the racket slice sideways? Then there'll be spin on the ball—which means that it's going to bounce to your right. That is, if it's on your backhand it will bounce in toward you; if it's on your forehand it will bounce out away from you. This little trick of anticipation soon gets to be second nature, and you'll anticipate automatically without thinking about it, once you've learned to pay attention to the server's racket.

When a soft second serve floats in like a marshmallow, don't get over eager. Many errors are made in returning too easy second serves. If you try to pulverize one, you'll hurry your swing, spoil your timing, snap your wrist, jerk at the ball, ruin your follow-through, and send your return on an unpredictable course.

Even the big pros seldom hit thunderbolts except on service and an occasional overhead smash. So move in on that soft serve a little more slowly, and put the ball where you want it with a graceful flowing stroke. (If your backhand isn't yet graceful and flowing, see the next chapter.)

· One last word. Confidence makes a big difference in returning service.

Many players await a serve with all-too-familiar feelings of insecurity, inferiority, ineptitude, and plain old fear. It gets to be a conditioned reflex, just as a fugitive quails whenever he hears a police siren.

Even after you've rooted out your faults such as wrong stance, wrong racket position, and taking your eye off the ball, you still may have to overcome that deep-seated lack of confidence. So psyche yourself up, if necessary. Remind yourself that by consistently sending back your opponent's serves, you are taking the edge off his most important weapon. He no longer can count on winning half the set almost automatically.

Fortify these thoughts with a bit of self-hypnosis. Silently tell yourself over and over again, I'll watch the ball and hit it well, I'll watch the ball and hit it well . . .

7 / Backhand Is Easy

You'll Learn to Like It

I can see the sneer on your face now. "So the backhand is easy, is it?" you're saying. "Okay, bub. Show me. Show me why it's easy. All I know is, I've been trying for years and I still can't hit a good backhand. What's so easy about it?"

A good many mediocre players have said that to me, in substance, at the club where I'm pro. And they've lived to enjoy their backhand so much that they run around balls to hit them on that side instead of their forehand.

Why? Because once you learn it, a backhand really is more fun to hit, gives you more power, gives you more control, and goes haywire less often than a forehand. You don't believe me yet. But you will.

Among the champions of the last twenty years, almost the only ones I can think of who preferred the forehand to the backhand are Kramer, Drobny, Sedgman, Trabert, Segura, Laver and Mulloy. Of these you can hardly count Drobny and Laver, because the former is a left-hander and the latter hits his own special brand of two-handed forehand. Practically all the others have found that, when they had trouble with their game, it was their forehand that gave them the trouble. The backhand stayed good when everything else turned sour. And, on good days or bad, it was always the backhand they liked for power drives, as well as for retrieving hard-to-get balls and for maneuvering an opponent around the court.

I'll grant you that a backhand is harder to acquire than a forehand. It doesn't come as easily. Any right-hander starting to learn tennis finds it natural to hit balls on his right side, not his left. Most club players develop a fair-to-middling forehand in the natural course of events. But their back-hand seldom comes naturally.

Which leads us to a paradox. The backhand, once learned, is really a more natural stroke. It's harder to acquire, but easier to keep. It's unnatural if you're a novice, but natural if you're trained.

When you're dealing cards, do you deal them backhand or forehand? When you toss your hat toward a hat rack, do you toss it backhand or forehand? When you slap your enemy in the face with a glove, in order to challenge him to a duel, do you slap backhand or forehand?

The answer, if you're normal, is backhand. The backhand is the natural way to do lots of things. So don't try to insist that it has to be unnatural in tennis.

Once you learn the backhand drive, you'll be amazed at how easy it becomes for you. That's because you'll be driving with your body out of the way, instead of driving across your body as you must in a forehand.

Suppose you're running to the side to retrieve your opponent's shot. If you're running to your right sideline, your torso is in your way as you make the forehand drive; your body is between your arm and the ball. But if you're running toward your left sideline, what a difference! As you hit that backhand, your body is behind your arm, completely out of the way.

Or suppose you're racing back toward your baseline. You're trying to catch up with a ball that has gone beyond you. If you catch it, you'll have to start your stroke while your back is toward the net. Now, if that ball is to your right as you run back, all you have to do is swat it with a simple backhand motion, turning your trunk and shoulders to your right as you follow through. Just a simple, natural movement. But it's not nearly so simple if the ball is at your left as you run back toward it. This time, when you hit it, you have to reach across your body. You have to return it over your left shoulder, and it's almost impossible to get any of your weight into such a stroke. Try these two maneuvers sometime, when you're rallying, and even if your backhand isn't at all accurate you'll still find that you can put your weight into the backhand but not the forehand.

Why are the most deadly blows in judo dealt backhanded? Because it's much easier to put power behind a backhand. Why are backhanded punches illegal in boxing? Because they can hurt a fighter too severely. Give yourself a demonstration the next time you want to hit something with your fist. Whether you're slapping a punching bag or knocking over a table lamp, you'll find that you can do it harder with a backhander. Just the feeling in your hand and shoulder will prove it to you.

"All right," you're growling, "but let's get back to tennis. Why isn't my backhand tennis drive as easy and natural as my other backhand motions?"

For one simple reason. In dealing cards or backhanding a punching bag or doing any of the other things just mentioned, you let your elbow stay close to your body. That's where it feels natural, in a backhand motion. And that's where it should be.

But not in tennis! In tennis, if you keep your elbow close to your body, you usually slice the ball out the sideline. You can't get your weight into the drive. That cramped elbow makes you poke or flick at the ball. It makes you hit inside the ball, instead of meeting it squarely.

Out with the Elbow!

The common fault of most poor players, in hitting their backhand, is that they let the ball pass too close to them as they drive. Which is simply another way of saying that they hit with their elbow too close to their body. Their elbow is bent; it should be straight.

The right way to hit a backhand is with your whole arm extended. Not stiff, just extended naturally, with the elbow as straight as it is when you let your hand drop to your side.

This is the first thing to concentrate on, when you begin polishing up your backhand. Think about standing well away from the ball when you hit it so that your elbow has to be straight instead of bent. Your racket should meet the ball when it is about even with your right hip (instead of even with your belt buckle as for the forehand) and four to four and a half feet away from you. This won't be too easy. You'll have to work on yourself a while before you can break the habit of standing close to the path of the ball. Sometimes you'll even have to back away toward the sideline a little when you're learning in order to get enough daylight between your belt buckle and the ball.

The best position for your feet, as you probably know, is with toes pointing toward the sideline. The best way to hold the racket is to take it in the eastern grip, as described in Chapter 4, and then give the racket an eighth-circle turn to the right. That's the eastern backhand grip. Your palm is now on top of the edge of the handle instead of flat against the side. Your thumb can be either along the edge or curled under. Of course you'll hit the ball with the opposite face of the racket from the one that meets the ball on the forehand.

Figure 7. The eastern backhand grip.

It's Done with Mirrors

A good way to brush up your backhand is to use a mirror. Stand in front of a full-length glass and make your stroke over and over. This helps a lot in breaking down your bad habits and replacing them with good ones.

To start, stroke through your forehand a few times. Make it smooth and flowing, with a long follow-through, as I drummed into you earlier in this book. Now, while you're still repeating that forehand drive, let your left hand rest on the racket too. As your left hand moves along the same path as your right, it will be following just about the path that it would if you were a lefthanded player hitting a backhand. In other words, the racket should do almost precisely the same thing in either a forehand or a backhand.

That's why it will help you a little to let your left hand rest beside your right, as if you were holding a baseball bat, for a few moments while you keep practicing your forehand in front of the mirror. Now, still repeating that stroke, take your right hand away from the racket and let your left do the whole thing. Watch yourself in the mirror. It will give you a good picture of how your backhand should look.

So much for your preliminary. Now grip the racket in your right hand again, face the mirror, and start practicing your backhand. Imagine that your right hip is toward the net, as it should be, so that the mirror gives you the same view you'd get if you were watching yourself from the sideline.

Make your stroke slowly at first. Keep concentrating on that elbow. Straighten it out. Get your racket away from your body.

Then take a look at your racket as you draw it back to start the swing. Where does it pause, just before starting forward again? It should be somewhere low, between your knee and hip, not up around your left ear where so many players persist in pulling it.

Another thing about that backswing: Make it rhythmic. Let it flow. Your racket should come back and start forward again all as part of the same movement. Too many players draw the racket back and hold it there, destroying the rhythm of the shot, before they begin their drive. Your racket should travel at the same speed through all parts of the shot—the drawback, the drive itself, and the follow-through. No jerky drawback. No acceleration as you meet the ball. There are no sudden movements of a good player's racket. He may be sprinting at breakneck speed, he may be diving headlong for the ball, but his racket never jerks or pokes. It always swings smoothly. Keep reminding yourself of that when you're playing: *no sudden movements.*

All right. You're still swinging your racket back and forth in front of the mirror, practicing your backhand drive, keeping it slow and fluid and graceful. Think about your right knee for a moment. Is it bent as you hit? It should be. But the average player's knee isn't.

Too many players hit a backhand more or less stiff-legged, particularly when they've absorbed the first idea that they must stand well away from the ball while hitting it. In the effort to keep themselves back from the ball, and to keep their elbow straight, they unconsciously straighten their knees too.

Loosen up. Bend your knees, the right one more than the left. Keep them flexible. And keep them bent as you follow through.

This knee business isn't as trivial as it seems. It's a basic point. Here's why.

Your whole follow-through depends on good knee action. If your knee is stiff, you'll automatically lean in the wrong direction as you hit and follow through. You'll lean away from the net instead of toward it. This ruins a backhand.

You should take a long sweeping follow-through, ending with the racket at arm's length away from you and beyond your right hip. The face of the racket should be perpendicular to the ground, like a coin standing on edge. But more important even than the position of your racket is the position of your body. You must be leaning into the ball—leaning toward the net.

Day after day, hour after hour, on every club court or public court I've ever watched, I've seen players rear back as they hit a backhand. It's fatal. Look at yourself in the mirror. Which way are you leaning as you follow through? If you're leaning backward—or falling backward, which is even more common in actual play—you're hitting late, and the ball is almost certain to sail into the next court.

Blissful Backhands

These workouts with a mirror will help you on the court. Of course they won't do the whole job. There are some things about a backhand that you can learn only by actually hitting the ball, over and over again.

Even when you've perfected a smooth, graceful stroke before the mirror, you're likely to have trouble on the court for a while in meeting the ball correctly. Your mirror practice won't entirely cure you of the habit of bellying up too close to the ball as you hit it. You'll still find yourself stroking with a bent elbow and meeting the ball only a foot or two in front of your abdomen, until you've practiced a while with a ball.

Even Don Budge, whose backhand is the greatest of this era, was troubled for a long time by hitting inside the ball—which meant that he was too close to it. He continually sliced the ball out the sideline. When he finally began to concentrate on hitting outside the ball—thus making himself extend his arm to almost its full length—he got the booming backhand that made him famous.

In your own league you can do the same thing. When you begin meeting the ball properly, at arm's length and leaning into it, you'll hit it like a rifle shot and yet you won't be exerting yourself at all. A smooth, flowing stroke which puts your weight into the drive is the whole trick.

You'll find yourself really enjoying your backhand shots instead of dreading them. More and more you'll favor the backhand side, as most good players do. Remember that Billie Jean King became the world's champion with a forehand that did not equal her classic backhand, that Jan Kodes won Wimbledon with the same weakness, that John Newcombe won at Forest Hills with a forehand that was vulnerable. Get a good backhand, and your forehand shots will take care of themselves.

8 / When You're Off Form

What to Do If You're Losing

It's one of those days when nothing seems to work. Your first serve won't go in, and your second is a luscious, fat clay pigeon for the enemy. Your drives are misbehaving, your timing is off when you try to volley, your backhand has turned completely sour. Worse yet, your opponent is having a diabolically good day. He's on. He's sharp. He's murdering you.

So you're getting madder and madder.

Furthermore, you're beginning to feel badly tired. You're winded. Your hand trembles a little when you grasp the racket. Your feet hurt.

It all adds up to the hateful fact that you're taking a trimming from somebody you know you can beat. Is there anything you can do about it? Plenty!

The first thing to do: Stop looking mad.

Stop scowling or growling when you miss a shot. Take a deep breath, relax and get a grip on yourself, and make up your mind not to let your opponent see the slightest sign that you're angry or frustrated.

Maybe you're still boiling inwardly, maybe the top of your head is going to blow off any instant—never mind. Conceal it. Be an actor. Wear a mask. When you flub an easy shot, chuckle!

This is a form of psychological war against your opponent. Every time he sees you tear your hair, it encourages him. Your screams are music in his ears. He actually plays better because of the knowledge that you are baffled and maddened. He gains confidence, loosens up a little, and his strokes automatically get smoother.

Therefore, you shouldn't give him the satisfaction of seeing your dismay. Play it smart. Look confident and unworried. Imagine you're Jack

Kramer, playing dismally and trailing by two sets against Frankie Parker in the 1947 finals at Forest Hills, yet still certain of victory. Just as Kramer's serene grin shook Parker's confidence, so you can make your opponent wonder "What kind of powerhouse is that guy? Why isn't he worried? What's he getting ready to pull out of the hat?"

You'll be amazed to see how it bothers your opponent when you laugh at your own poor shot, when you aren't worried by his best efforts. One of the reasons why Fred Perry became champion of the world was that he guffawed wholeheartedly when he lost a crucial point. His amusement unsettled the other man. Perry always seemed so assured even when losing, always seemed to be having so much fun during the most grueling test of endurance, that no one facing him could ever feel confident.

If you can't laugh when the tide of battle is running against you, at least you can put on a poker face. Try it. Just become expressionless, gestureless, unspeaking. Coolly ignore your opponent. Make like a machine.

You'll find that it gets on his nerves. It does in any sport. Joe Louis frightened other fighters with his deadpan concentration. He didn't even blink when they hit him hard—so they got an idea it was useless to try to hurt him. Paavo Nurmi's cold, calm, unstrained face in the midst of the hottest foot races made rival runners tie up a little because they noticed he wasn't worried when they passed him.

Ben Hogan was called "Little Ice Water" and was dreaded by the top tournament golfers of the world. "He seems inhuman," a pro said once. "He makes you kind of uneasy and you start to foozle your shots." Before one big tourney, a great golfer remarked, "Look at that Mangrum. Steady as a rock. Even grins once in a while. But if Hogan were in this tournament, you'd see Lloyd shake when he lit a cigarette. I'm telling you, the guy's got ulcers, and Ben Hogan gave them to him."

Remember how Helen Wills—"Little Poker Face"—rattled her rivals? Not only was she completely unworried by them, but she was completely unconscious of their existence. In changing courts on the odd games, Helen usually passed within a few feet of the other woman, but never spoke. Never even glanced at her. Just behaved as if there were nobody in sight. It gave Helen Jacobs, and other female stars, an inferiority complex when playing against Helen Wills that held them back for years. Chris Evert is almost as deadpan. Among the male stars, Ken Rosewall shows that same icy unconcern.

Such tactics will work for you too—perhaps not to the point of setting your opponent all a-tremble, but probably to the point of bothering him and making him tighten up a bit. More important, this strategy will improve your own game.

Yes, that's what I said! Your own game will really improve, just through the mere act of concealing your anger or dismay. You'll be surprised to find yourself making fewer errors, and even feeling less tired.

Just try this the next time your game is off and you feel your blood pressure skyrocketing. Conceal all signs of anger. Either act the part of the laughing champion, amused by a temporary streak of errors—like Fred Perry—or else just turn cool and unworried—like Helen Wills. Either way, just by dissembling, by pretending that you're not the least bit mad, you'll feel less mad inwardly.

It Pays to Be Phlegmatic

The more calmness you pretend, the more you'll feel. It's a strange psychological fact, known to anybody who has ever dabbled in amateur theatricals, that every actor tends to "live" the role he's acting. If he plays the part of a calm man, he feels calm. That's just as true on a tennis court as it is on a stage.

You can't stay angry inside if you're chuckling externally. When you concentrate on looking serene and unworried, you automatically quiet down behind your belt buckle. Whenever you grin, you just can't help feeling better.

Thus, by the simple trick of putting up a calm front you do yourself a lot of good. You lower your blood pressure—literally and physically lower it. You quiet your nerves. Any doctor will tell you that anger is usually bad for your body, and that calm is good. The physiological wear and tear on a tennis player who lets himself get mad is sometimes downright dangerous. The blood pounds in his head, he feels sick to his stomach, his heart overworks, his reflexes get jerky. The greatest champion can't play good tennis when he's enraged.

That's why practically everybody who ever got to the top in tennis learned, early on the upward trip, that calmness is a must. Nobody who wants to win tennis matches can afford to get mad. I've seen youngsters in their early teens stomping and shaking their heads and yelling at themselves when they miss points; and I've seen those same youngsters as calm as Mongolians during fierce tennis duels a few years later. Jack Kramer was known to throw his racket over the fence when he was playing in the under-fifteen age bracket. But nobody ever saw him so much as bite his lip during an adult match. The same with Riggs, Budge (in spite of his red hair), Vines, Tilden, and all the rest. Tilden used to put on a great show of anger at linesmen or umpire occasionally, but it was always a calculated act to gain himself a breathing space or to intimidate the official into calling the next close ones in his favor. Few people ever saw Tilden get mad at himself or at his doubles partner.

You hurt yourself in all kinds of ways when you lose your temper in tennis. Not only do you damage yourself physically, and wreck your timing and stroking, but you degrade yourself in the eyes of your acquaintances. I remember an afternoon when one star had a series of tantrums while playing against me in the finals of a southern tournament. He kicked up such a row that various linesmen and umpires were quitting at intervals, and quite a number of replacements had to be made. Finally he got so enraged at missing a shot that he smashed the ball into the grandstand, hitting a woman. Luckily she was hit only on the arm, but her escort had to be forcibly restrained from invading the court and loosening a few of the star's teeth.

By the time the match ended, this player was so sick with rage, frustration, and shame that he couldn't even eat supper. He's never been invited back to that tournament since. Nor has he been fully forgiven by friends who saw his exhibition that day. It's a shame, because he is normally a nice fellow—and he might have become the national champion if his bursts of temper hadn't handicapped him.

Check Up on Yourself

Well, let's get back to this bad day you're having. We'll assume that you're now imperturbable in the face of disaster, but that your strokes still aren't working well. What to do?

The thing to do is to start analyzing yourself. Run through a mental check list of the mistakes that cause erratic stroking. You've read about those mistakes in Chapter 2. Review them in your mind while you're playing and you'll probably realize what's wrong.

Are you hitting too hard? That's a common fault when the game goes badly. Stop pressing. Hit a little easier, and your control will improve. It's better just to keep getting the ball back, with medium pace, than to wallop a bullet drive that goes outside.

Are you keeping your eye on the ball? Even the best players have to remind themselves, sometimes, about watching that ball. Keep your eye on it—not only while you're hitting it but while your opponent is hitting it. Whenever you glance away from that moving pellet, your accuracy suffers.

Are you "feeling" the ball as you hit it? If not, concentrate on hitting "through" the ball, with a long, easy follow-through in the path you want it to follow.

Are you relaxed? Tenseness not only makes you jerk your strokes but tires you. Think about stroking with a smooth, fluid, rhythmic motion—everything easy, nothing tense. After each point, while you're walking into position for the next, walk slowly. And put your mind on various muscles, one after another. Loosen up your calf muscles, your thigh muscles, and your hips while you walk, so that you're ambling instead of bustling. How about your stomach muscles? Are they tightened up? Let go. Is there tenseness somewhere in your back or shoulders? Relax it. Quit clenching your fist. Quit clamping your teeth. Quit knitting your brow, or stiffening your neck. Just go over yourself mentally, from toes to scalp and back again, making yourself limp all over. You're likely to find that this will take the kinks out of your game.

Another way to check up on yourself is to ask someone to watch and tell you what you're doing wrong. This often has startling results, even when the observer doesn't open his mouth.

Time after time, at the club where I coach, somebody groans, "Bob, for the love of mercy, watch me for a few strokes, will you? I'm doing something wrong, but I don't know what it is." So I'll watch. And almost invariably the player's next strokes are beautiful.

It's odd but true that when you know someone is analyzing your movements you make those movements more carefully. You pay more attention to form—and consequently your form improves. Try this trick on yourself when you have a tennis-wise friend on the sidelines. Get him to study your form, and you'll immediately begin playing better tennis—or else there's something so glaringly wrong with your stroke that the friend will probably spot it at once.

Put on the Brakes

Here's another general rule that will always be helpful when you're doing poorly:

Slow down.

Fight a delaying action. Take every pause you're ethically entitled to. Let Father Time play a little on your side.

You've often seen a basketball or football team call time out when the opposition began to get the upper hand. You've seen a fighter go into a clinch when he was hurt. You've seen smart lawyers move for adjournments and postponements and delays when a trial was developing badly for their client. In practically every field of human activity, it's good strategy to do a little stalling when you're in trouble.

In tournament tennis, there are some successful players who carry this strategy beyond the bounds of good sportsmanship. They repeatedly call halts to tie a shoelace, or tighten their belts, or pick up a tiny scrap of paper from the court. There are long pauses while they towel their faces or sip a glass of water. They "accidentally" kick a ball far out of court so that everyone has to wait while a ball boy retrieves it. They stop everything for a long argument with the umpire.

I'd advise you not to use such tactics if you want to keep the friendship of your opponent, or the respect of spectators. This flagrant stalling is considered definitely unethical in club tennis. Instead you can slow down the general tempo of the game by perfectly legitimate means. There'll be no long delays, but a series of fractional pauses which will add up to the leisure you need to recover your breath, collect your wits, and give your muscles extra moments of relaxation. An extra second or two between every play can make a big difference in your game. It can smooth out your strokes and eliminate errors.

When you walk over to pick up a ball, walk slowly. Stroll.

When you walk into position to receive service, walk slowly. Never mind if your opponent is waiting impatiently. Let him wait. Take your time.

When it's your turn to serve, don't be brisk. Don't hurry to get to that baseline. And when you get there, take a leisurely look down at your feet to make sure you're toeing the line. (Too many club players just hustle back and serve from the general vicinity of the line, without even glancing down at it.) Take a last peek at your opponent to make sure he's ready to receive.

When you change courts on the odd game, give yourself a real breathing space. You shouldn't dawdle, but you can saunter. Walk as if you have plenty of time—which you have. Stop at the net and give your face and neck a thorough mopping.

By slowing down at all these intervals, you imperceptibly change the rhythm of the match. You relax your muscles and quiet your nerves. Gradually you'll find yourself hitting with smoother, easier strokes—controlling the ball better—giving your opponent more trouble.

When You're Tired

This business of slackening speed between points is sound tactics at any stage of a match when you're making too many errors, or dropping behind in the score. Naturally, it's doubly sound when you feel tired. Even if you're playing beautifully, and leading, you should slow down a little if your feet are starting to drag.

It won't be often, however, that you'll feel tired when the game is going your way. The kind of weariness that attacks most players on a tennis court is more emotional, and mental, than it is physical. Ever notice the difference between the winner and loser of a tough, closely fought match? The winner bounces off the court full of ginger and high spirits. The loser can hardly drag himself to the showers.

Likewise, you've probably noticed the difference in yourself after winning and losing. It's only when you've taken a trimming that you feel too tired to hold your head up through the evening. When you've won, even if the match was long and hard, you usually feel fairly good, don't you?

This is something for you to remember in the middle of a hot set that's going against you. When your control is erratic and your muscles are tired, you can fortify yourself with the knowledge that your tired feeling is partly mental, and that you'll be feeling better as soon as you get your game under control. This knowledge will help you to forget about Old Man Fatigue and concentrate on the little tricks already described in this chapter to put yourself back in the groove.

However, there comes a moment in every tennis player's life when he is genuinely and unmistakably footsore, winded, and spent. After too many sets, at too advanced an age, you'll feel a ton or two of lead in your muscles no matter how well the game is going. The only sane thing to do, when this moment comes, is to call a halt. You've had enough tennis for the day. If you want to live to play another day, knock off for now, head for the shower and the easy chair, and postpone further tennis until tomorrow or next weekend.

Believe me, brother, this is important. When you feel badly tired, call it a day. I've seen more than one player who thought he had a perfectly sound heart drop dead on the court because he didn't know when to stop. If you're over thirty-five, quit kidding yourself that you can go like a college boy.

There are milder stages of fatigue, however, and you can adjust your game to take care of them. If you're in the closing stages of a match that's important to you, and you feel your energy ebbing away, here's what to do about conserving it.

You have a choice of two courses of action: you can shorten the rallies, or you can give yourself longer intervals to rest.

The way to shorten the rallies is to hit harder. Make the ball zip. Try for aces. Make every shot a forcing shot if you can.

Obviously this is a big gamble. We spent a lot of time in Chapter 2 on the reasons why you *shouldn't* hit harder. You have less margin for safety, less ability to control the ball, when you try to murder it. But now, with your strength running out, with the odds lengthening against you, it may be smart to stake everything on a quick plunge. Your chances of winning are better in a short set than in a long set. Settle every rally with one or two wallops, finish every game quickly, and you'll be getting maximum value from what stamina you have remaining.

Your other possible course of action, giving yourself an extra instant of rest after each stroke, can be accomplished by making your drives slower and higher. That way the ball takes longer to reach your opponent, and you get an additional split second or so to relax between shots.

This is the less drastic of the two gambles. By hitting softer drives that clear the net by several feet instead of several inches, you're not staking the point on one risky shot, as you do in the other strategy of shortening the rallies. Your temperament will probably determine which technique you use to ward off exhaustion. If you're the plunger type, you'll probably go all-out for a quick decision. If you're more conservative, and prefer to play it safe, you'll simply slow down the speed of the ball and husband your strength while waiting for the other fellow to make errors.

It goes without saying that you'll do as little running as possible, meanwhile making your opponent do a lot. The multitude of ways to manage this are all covered in various parts of this book. In fact, the general theme of this whole volume might be stated as "How to use your head to save your legs." Therefore, I'm assuming that you'll use all the tennis wisdom you acquire in the rest of this book, and summon all the tricks of strategy listed in it, to outmaneuver your opponent. In the clutch, when you're tired and victory hangs in the balance, all these principles of court position are doubly important. I won't repeat them here. I'll simply remind you that the most important tactic, when you're tired, is this:

Hit down the line on your forehand, and cross-court on your backhand.

One reason for this strategy is to keep the ball on your opponent's backhand, which is almost certain to be weaker than his forehand. Another reason is that you'll find it considerably easier to put your backhand shots across court than down the line. I won't go into the mechanics of it here but simply assure you that you can hit better backhands, and get less tired, when you aim for your opponent's backhand corner. A little experimenting should convince you that this is true. The same principle holds in reverse for your forehand. A forehand down the line is a much easier shot than a forehand cross-court. Even as world amateur champ, Jack Kramer never had a good forehand cross-court. He didn't develop one until he turned pro. Then he worked out with me, a half hour daily all throughout the fall before his pro series with Riggs began, hitting nothing but cross-court forehands. It isn't an easy shot to master, even for a worldbeater like Jack. And when you're tired, it's plain poison.

Still another reason for the strategy suggested above is that it involves less running for you. Look at Figure 1. You've just hit the ball from your forehand side and slanted it across into your opponent's forehand corner. Now look what he can do. He can hammer it straight down the line and you'll have to run like a fiend to intercept it. Or, if you try to take the net behind your drive, he also has the choice of dinking a shallow, sharply angled cross-court ball past your forehand as you run in. Your body is moving to your left as you invade the forecourt on this exchange—and, if you try to lunge to your right while moving to your left, you'll find it's no cinch. That's why it's sheer stupidity for any ordinary player to try to rush the net behind his cross-court forehand.

I could name other advantages of this strategy, but three ought to be enough. Whatever else you do, whatever you forget, always remember that when you're tiring you should keep putting the ball down the line on your forehand, and cross-court on your backhand.

9 / When You're Overmatched

Break Up His Game

It happens to everybody sometime. And now it's happened to you. You're in there against a much better player, and he's wiping the court with you. This is a match you really want to win, so you're keyed up to a great effort, and your game is sharper than usual, but still you're being overpowered. What to do?

In this kind of situation, the average club player just grinds his teeth and plays harder, without any change in style. So the match continues uneventfully until his beating is completed. Worse yet, he plays exactly the same kind of game, next time he tackles the same opponent, and takes another beating by about the same score. He may go on year after year, losing to the same man in the same way, without ever trying any new tactics on him.

But you're different, I trust. If you were dumb you wouldn't be reading this book. You consider tennis a battle of wits as well as rackets, and when you can't outstroke an opponent you'll try to outmaneuver him.

So now the question arises, how can you think your way through to victory against somebody whose normal game is superior to yours?

The answer is to prevent him from playing his normal game. Throw him off stride. Start him guessing. Make him use strokes he doesn't like to use, play in parts of the court he prefers to avoid, switch to faster or slower tempo.

Of course, this is going to make the game tougher and trickier for you as well as for him. To force him into changing his style, you've got to change yours first. Playing differently is going to mean pain and strain, at least mentally. So it comes down to a choice. How about it? Would you rather play out the match, in your usual comfortable pattern, and get beaten—or make a great effort to pull the pattern apart, for the sake of a chance to win? In other words, are you willing to try a more difficult style in order to come out on top?

How to Stop a Net-Stormer

Let's say your opponent has a vicious net game. You can't dislodge him from the forecourt. He's got better anticipation than Jack Kramer, he volleys like a Garand rifle, and he's slaying you.

Okay. You've tried many times to pass him at the net and it hasn't worked. So you've got to drive him away from the net. There are several ways you can do it.

One way is to get to the net before he does. Once you're in the forecourt, he'll be a fool indeed to rush in there himself. Maybe you're rather slow on your feet and afraid to try a net blitz for that reason. Never mind. You don't have to run fast to take the net. Just send over a slow, arching drive that clears the net by several feet. While it's in the air, you'll have plenty of time to meander forward.

Or send up a skyscraper lob. This is a tactic that you seldom see in club tennis—there seems to be some notion among club players that only sissies lob—but the tournament sharks use it all the time. Tilden could and would keep the ball high in the air against anybody who bothered him at the net. Riggs broke up Budge's net game the same way. Try it yourself. The results may surprise you pleasantly.

The lob is really a three-pronged weapon. It can be used to force your opponent back from the net. Or it can give you time to take the net yourself. Or, without even using it, you can make it a threat (after you actually have used it a few times) to prevent the opposition from crowding the net so closely.

Maybe he's rushing the net behind his own serve. Your answer, then, is to stand closer to receive his serve, particularly when it's in your forehand court. Most players stay too far back when they're receiving. Move in! Keep your eye on the ball, and you'll be able to hit it in time. By hitting it sooner, you'll get it back to the server sooner, and he'll have less time to run forward. Furthermore, you'll be hitting the ball while it's higher in the air, and this will give you a better angle to fire it at his feet as he rushes in.

Maybe he's not coming in with his serve, but biding his time until he gets a short drive from you. Then he takes it on the run and follows in for a kill. Okay. Study his style a little. Does he come in behind a backhand drive, or a forehand? Undoubtedly he prefers one to the other. So keep the ball on the side he doesn't prefer, when you have to hit a shorter drive than usual. Keep placing the ball as shrewdly as possible, aim closer to the sidelines, get as much length as you can; and you'll give him fewer chances to storm the net. Grab the net yourself when he hits a short drive, and he'll have fewer chances yet.

When he does come in, lob a few times. After he's chased a few high ones back to the baseline, he'll be more cautious (and probably more tired) so he won't advance quite as close to the net. This will give you a chance to try a few dink shots, right at his feet, when he comes into the forecourt. These little trickling teasers, which barely hop over the net and don't bounce high, are dynamite against a man who's in forecourt but not quite far enough into it. They make him spoon the ball up, giving you a soft, rising ball which you can come in and murder.

Another little trick that bothers a man at the net is for you to try a passing shot with considerable lift to it, so it sails just above his reach, preferably on his backhand side. This works best in doubles, but it can also be pretty potent in singles. Consider the geometry of it. If a man at the net wants to cover a low passing shot, he can lunge to the side, even throw himself headlong if necessary, and reach out horizontally to intercept the ball. But if the passing shot is a floater, he can't lean as far off the vertical and still reach high enough. Therefore his defense is narrowed when the ball is higher. Just try to touch a wall, standing at arm's length from it. If you stretch out your arm straight from the shoulder, you can touch the wall at that height. But if you try to touch it at a greater height, you have to stand closer to the wall—and as you stretch your body and lift your arm, you have a harder time keeping your balance. In the same way, if a man wants to stop a sideline floater, he has to be much nearer to its line of flight.

If He Outsteadies You

Let's take another situation. Let's assume you're being beaten by one of those Mechanical Marvels who just keep getting the ball back. His big asset is steadiness. He stays back, tries nothing spectacular, merely trades drives with you until you make an error.

You know you can't outsteady him. In every long rally you'll falter before he does. So you'll have to make your own points. You'll have to start forcing. Rush the net unexpectedly. Or make him come to the net, by feeding him short balls and drop shots.

Run him around a bit. Alternate long straight drives with short diagonal ones—the old Cochet system. Or gamble on some corner shots to pull him out of position. Hit some quick low lobs just to see what he does with them.

Or play feather-duster tennis a while. Soft shots often break up the rhythm of a smooth, steady stroker, and lead him into a string of errors. Give him some high, slow drives—semilobs that clear the net by six or seven feet.

Above all, though, move in on him. Hustle him. Step in closer to take his serves when they're on your forehand. Push forward when he drives and hit the ball on the rise. Crowd the net at every opportunity.

The reason for this is that you want to give him less time for his strokes. A steady player is usually one who takes long, graceful, flowing motions. If the ball comes at him sooner, from closer range, he doesn't have time to sweep his racket around so smoothly, and he may begin hooking it into the alley.

When He Finds Your Flaw

Here's another predicament. Suppose your opponent has found a fatal weakness in your game—your backhand, maybe—and is pounding it on every play. He's putting every ball on that tender spot of yours, and it's giving you fits.

Obviously you've got to prevent him from putting the ball there. How to do it? Eliminate rallies, and gamble on a quick decision for every point.

Just as Bobby Riggs would never rally with Don Budge, would never let him bring that booming backhand into play, you should never rally with somebody who's got you outgunned. Either bring him to the net, or take the net yourself, on every exchange.

Throw caution into the ashcan. You're getting beaten anyhow, so why shouldn't you take chances? If they don't pay off, you're in no worse a spot than you were already. So start slamming that ball hard, and aim it at the corners. When your shots go in, they'll be forcing shots, and you'll have your tormentor on the defensive for a change. He'll be scrambling to get the ball back at all, instead of taking dead aim at the chink in your armor.

At moments when he does get time to take aim, and all you can do is wait and pray, try a little of Jack Kramer's strategy. Kramer's forehand volley is much stronger than his backhand volley. So he deliberately leaves an opening on his forehand side, moving over too far to protect his vulnerable backhand. But he's watching that hole on his forehand side, and he's ready to jump that way the instant he sees his opponent aiming for it. Because the forehand is his strong side, he invites everyone to put the ball on that side. Try it for yourself. Coax your opponent into hitting to your strength instead of your weakness. Get yourself a little out of position, and stay on your toes for a quick jump when he steps into the trap.

Don't Slug with a Slugger

If you're confronting a man who hits the ball so hard that you can only wave to it as it goes by, don't try to match wallops with him. A hard driver always plays his best game against another hard driver. So stop feeding him hard drives, once you're convinced that his are harder. Instead, bring him up to the net with short balls, then pass him or lob over his head. If he hits a bullet drive, he probably isn't much of a net player, never having had to be, and he may go up like a balloon once you pull him out of the backcourt.

Remember this, too: he likes to haul off and belt the ball at about waist height. So don't let him. Don't give him waist-high balls. Give him slow, high balls that he'll have to club at shoulder level or higher. Many men would smack their lips at such shots, but he may have more trouble with them than he would with your hardest drives.

Another thing. A really hard hitter is almost invariably erratic. Ellsworth Vines, whose drives were the fastest in the history of the game, lost many matches to mediocre players. He lost by beating himself: he kept driving the ball out of court. Any lesser slugger will do the same thing—and do it oftener. A club player who powers the ball can almost be counted on to hit at least every third or fourth drive outside. So don't get rattled by his heavy artillery. If you'll just keep pushing the ball back somehow, and prolong the rally for a few shots, he'll usually make you a gift of the point.

How to Handle a "System" Player

A really powerful player often develops a lopsided game. He's so good in one department that he forgets about the others. He finds he can win with a beautifully simple system, so he sticks to it.

Smith's system is to bang the ball into one corner and then the other. That was all he needed. Newcombe's system is to blast over a big serve, rush the net, and climb aboard the return. Rosewall's is the long-and-short theory: hit a deep drive, then a shallow diagonal one, then grab the net while his opponent was in no-man's land or chasing a wide ball across the sideline. Nastase, weak off the ground, is always at the net. Richey plays a beautiful baseline game, shooting a steady stream of accurate drives down the lines.

Some of the best club players have this same tendency to groove their game. Very few are all-around, all-court players. They stick to two or three favorite shots, work you out of position with them, and finally ace you or force you into an error.

Let's say you're up against one of these formidable opponents. He's running you all over the court—from side to side, or forward and back. You know you've got to do something to break up his system, or he'll run you to death.

First of all, analyze his system. What's the pattern? What shots, or series of shots, is he using repeatedly? What are his favorite maneuvers?

Once you know this, you can begin to take the play away from him. Place your serves and returns more carefully, to avoid putting them where he likes them. Turn on the pressure, and start taking chances. Your only hope, against this kind of superior strength, is to be bold and reckless. Step up and paste the ball on the nose. Aim for the corners so he'll have to do the running for a change. Lob and take the net. Give him whatever shots he isn't used to.

Whenever he does get the upper hand and a rally falls back into its familiar pattern, don't kill yourself. Don't let him run you around until your tongue hangs out. If you see you can reach a ball only by sprinting like crazy, and you also see that he's waiting in position to cut off your return, let the ball go. Save your strength for the next point.

Try your opponent out on a low lob over his backhand shoulder. This is a tough one for almost everybody. And try him on some soft, shallow, low-bouncing balls to his backhand. A soft ball isn't always an easy one to return, even for experts. Jack Crawford of Australia, one of the great players of the thirties, lost the world's championship because opponents found he couldn't handle such shots.

Maybe you're playing a chop-stroke specialist. Some players can give you a lot of trouble by forever slicing and chopping the ball. Its bounce is bothersome. Your answer should be to jump in and volley those slices before they bounce. A slice is rising as it comes over the net, which makes it the easiest kind of ball to volley. Just punch it down for a placement.

Keep an Ace Up Your Sleeve

Way back in the early days of the century, there was a canny old competitor named Hackett who was surprisingly tough to beat in any big match. He was a diabolical psychologist. For example, sometimes he'd be up against some whirlwind player who began piling up a lead on him. Facing a beating, Hackett immediately eased up his own game so much that the match looked like a walkaway. Hackett's opponent had such an easy time of it, for a while, that he unconsciously let down. At that point he got a nasty surprise. He suddenly realized that Hackett's game had stiffened drastically, and the whole complexion of the match was changing. Often the victim of this psychological booby trap couldn't pick his own game up again, having let it relax, and Hackett surged from behind to win.

Whenever somebody gets really fat-headed with overconfidence, he can't play well. He just isn't able to lift his game to meet a sudden threat. Try this trick sometime when you're in there with somebody who has the Indian sign on you.

Another Hackett trick was to spot certain weaknesses in his opponent, and then just keep them in the back of his mind, doing nothing much about them. Then, only a few times during the match, when he needed points badly, he'd play to those weaknesses and get the point. This was a lot smarter than hammering the weak spot constantly, because the other man might change style and cover up the weakness. If you're in a close match with somebody, and you notice that his backhand is below par, let's say, maybe you'll be smarter to stab at that backhand once in a while, for a decisive point, than to aim a steady stream of balls at it. Then you have the advantage of surprise. A man who finds that every ball is coming to his backhand is going to be better prepared for those balls. He's going to keep edging over to protect his backhand. He's going to be ready to jump that way on every shot. And the continual practice on his backhand may strengthen it during the match.

Every competitive player with a weak backhand is used to having his backhand attacked. He's ready for it, expecting it, and he knows what to do about it. But suppose you keep aiming at his forehand corner instead. This will be something he wasn't expecting. The sheer novelty of having someone deliberately aim shots at his strong side may throw him a little off stride, draw him into a few errors. If so, those errors will really get under his skin. A man is used to finding his weakness weak—but if he finds his strength weak, he may get the shakes.

Even if he handles the forehand shots without trouble, you're still jockeying him into position for his downfall. He's feeling happy. He thinks either you don't realize his backhand is his secret sorrow, or else you just can't do anything about it. Then, when you've pulled him wide to his forehand, a backhand ball will be twice as hard for him to handle because he isn't ready for it. An occasional nip at his backhand, when he isn't edging over to protect it, ought to be good for a quick point.

Always play to weakness through strength. If a man is weak at the net, get him as far back behind the baseline as possible before you put your dink shot into the forecourt. If he's bad on lobs, wait until he's really on top of the net before you lob to him.

Remember Chapter 3, the one on anticipation? In a tough match where you're the underdog, try to save some of your anticipation for the clutches. If your opponent is tipping his hand, don't let him know that you see it. Here's what I mean:

I remember a match where one player had a habit of always returning anything on his backhand with a hard cross-court shot. Always. The other fellow soon noticed this. So what did he do? He began putting the ball to the backhand, then stepping up to the net with a broad confident grin and murdering the cross-court return, which was easy because he knew exactly where to station himself for it.

But the first player was no dummy. After this happened three or four times he saw why his opponent was grinning. He began mixing up his shots and wiped off the other man's grin in a hurry. Moral: When you learn how to anticipate one of your opponent's shots, try to keep your knowledge a secret from him and use it only when you want to pull yourself out of a hole.

Maybe you're playing someone who has a habit of driving to your forehand side, and changing to a chop when he wants to play your backhand. Lots of players do this. It's a glaring tip-off. But if you can keep him from realizing how glaring it is, you'll stand a better chance of beating him. When you see him cock his elbow for that chop, don't start moving to the left instantly, or he'll wonder how you knew where he was going to hit the ball. Pretty soon he'll catch on, and start aiming some of his chops at your forehand. Instead, start a little more slowly than you're capable of—slow enough so it isn't obvious you've got him tabbed, yet fast enough to get you there in time. Then, when a big point comes up, you can turn on extra pressure and start for the ball a lot sooner than he thought you could. If you do this just occasionally, instead of all the time, you can probably go through the whole match without letting him see that he's being played for a sucker.

In the middle of a fast rally, when you're being forced out of position, here are a couple of things that are handy to know.

If you've got to return a tough shot, and you're straining every sinew to get it over the net, remember that your chance is best if you aim it smack at the center of the net. You have the least chance if you try to skim it down the line. Here's why. A cross-court shot passes over a net about 3 feet high. A sideline shot passes over a net about 3 feet 5 inches high. You see, the net is higher by twice the diameter of the ball at the sideline. This is enough difference to catch many balls at the side that would have been good through the center.

If you have to run far out of court to retrieve the ball, there's one thing you need above all else: time. Time to get back into position. If you hit a hard, flat drive, you're helping your opponent. The faster your shot gets to him, the less time you'll have to run into position. A fast ball, returned fast, can go almost anywhere in the court and still ace you. So, when you're caught out of position, don't hit the ball hard unless you're taking a long-shot gamble on acing the other fellow. Instead, send it back slow and high and deep. By the time it comes down, you can be in court again, ready to keep the rally going. The seconds it takes a lob to climb high in the air and sink again are seconds when the clock is playing on your side.

There's a defense for every attack in tennis—and an attack to crack every defense—if you're shrewd enough to figure it out. Remember the basic rule: tactics consist of giving your enemy what he likes least. Maybe this means giving up some favorite weapons of your own. But you'd rather give them up than give up the match, wouldn't you? At least you'll have the initiative. You'll be making the other fellow dance to your music, instead of the other way round. You still may not beat him, but you'll worry him!

10 / Championship Doubles

Doubles is Different

Different strokes. Different speed. Different strategy. Even a different court. That's the doubles game, as compared to singles.

If I have my choice between singles and doubles, either to play or to watch, I'll take doubles every time. So will nearly everybody else. For the players, a four-handed game is more sociable and more interesting because it's a battle of wits with an infinite variety of possible plays. For spectators, doubles is exciting, spectacular, fast-changing.

In singles, the power player has a commanding advantage. But in doubles, finesse beats power; the bullet drive and the cannonball serve are almost useless; two slower but craftier players can often smother a pair of sluggers who'd have it all their own way on a singles court. That's why the vast multitude of average players, who are intelligent but not powerful, always get more fun out of doubles.

However, they don't get as much fun as they should. They'd enjoy doubles more if they understood it better.

The average game of social doubles is just four people trying to play singles on a doubles court. No strategy, and very little teamwork. They tire themselves out with needless running, and they sometimes blow a gasket because of annoyance with a partner or sheer frustration at the way their fastest shots boomerang.

There's a widespread delusion at tennis clubs and public courts that doubles is approximately the same game as singles. And then there's the old-fashioned idea, gradually dying out but dying hard, that the ideal strategy in doubles is for one player to cover the forecourt and the other to cover the backcourt. There's even a third delusion, among slightly more sophisticated players who have seen some topflight doubles but misunderstood it, that the idea for both players is to rush the net at every chance and pulverize the ball on every shot.

That third theory is only half wrong. The other two are completely wrong.

Doubles is first of all a game of diplomacy. It's no sport for individualists or stormy petrels. Anybody who gets mad at an erring partner is cutting his own throat in doubles. Even a dirty look or a cold shoulder invariably makes a bad situation worse. It's strange how many once-a-week doubles players have never grasped this simple principle of human relations.

Put it this way. Imagine yourself in your partner's place. You never enjoy being criticized, do you? You never like to be on the receiving end of a scowl or a deep-freeze treatment. It just makes you mad. Whenever you're mad you play erratic tennis. You probably try to slap the stuffing out of the ball—a sure way to lose control of it, and an even more certain path to defeat in doubles than in singles because a hard-hit ball frequently leaves you at the mercy of your opponents.

Therefore, it ought to be obvious that you shouldn't get mad, and you shouldn't make your partner mad. When your partner hits a poor shot, encourage him, don't bite his head off. He's doing the best he can. He doesn't make errors intentionally. He probably feels annoyed enough already, when he flubs one, without taking any mouth from you.

When a pitcher gets in trouble in a baseball game, the catcher strolls out to the mound to reassure him and calm him and encourage him. Not to snarl at him. Maybe the whole infield gathers around him. Do they call him names, or gaze upon him with silent contempt? Of course not. They pat him on the back. They remind him of his previous successes. They point out all the reasons why he'll be able to pull himself out of the present difficulty. By their tone of voice, and their facial expressions, and every gesture and remark, they do everything possible to convince this demoralized pitcher that they're his firm friends and staunch supporters. This is a tried-and-true technique in baseball—and in big-time tennis. The top doubles players never growl or scowl at each other, no matter what the provocation. But the irascible duffers in tennis clubs always ruin a doubles match—just as they do a bridge game—by giving in to their own tempers.

Different Strategy

Let's consider the strategy of doubles as it is played in modern championship competition. Probably you haven't the strokes of the champions, and never will have. But if you understand the champions' strategy, you'll get some ideas that will help you in your own league. Later in this book we'll analyze doubles as played in the strictly-for-fun brackets. But right now you need to lay some groundwork. You need to learn what doubles is really all about.

The objective of doubles strategy, whether in a Davis Cup match or on a backyard court, is to get command of the net.

In doubles practically all points are won at the net. Many singles matches are won from the baseline, but no doubles matches. Your whole aim in doubles should be to get to the net, and then make your opponents give you a rising ball which you can hit down. It's rather like volleyball. The whole idea is to "spike" the ball—hammer it down where the enemy can't handle it. To do this, you have to get up close.

Get the idea? Okay. Once you've grasped this cornerstone principle, you're ready to learn the other principles based on it.

Now, since your aim is to get to the net, what kind of serve should you use? A fast, hard one? Definitely not. If you put over a sledge-hammer serve, you won't have time to get into the forecourt before the ball comes back. Unless your serve is an ace or unreturnable, the return will catch you in that no-man's land between the baseline and the service line—which means that the ball will be at your feet and you'll have a hellish time trying to return it. Smart doubles players aim for their opponent's feet. Never let your own feet become such an easy target as they are when you hit a fast serve and then start forward.

In big-league doubles, the American twist serve is the standard one. That's the serve that arches over the net approximately head high, then drops sharply because of its topspin, and kicks wide to the side. Because it travels more slowly, the server has more time to get up to the net before the receiver can return the ball.

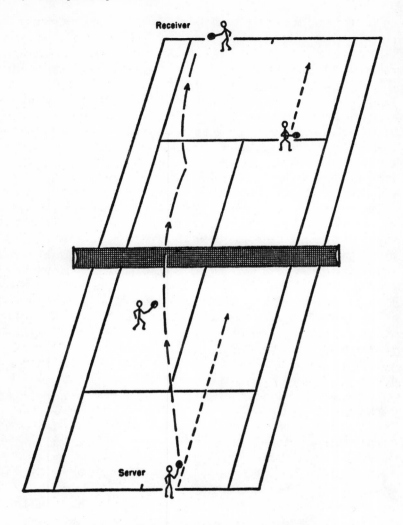

Figure 8. Position of all four players at the instant server hits his serve.

You seldom see a smashing, crashing serve in good doubles, even by the powerhouses such as Gonzales, Newcombe, or Smith. They know better. The only time they hit a cannonball is when they want to break up an opponent's rhythm. Sometimes a player gets used to returning the twist, because of steady practice at it during the match, and therefore the server feeds him an occasional low, flat ball just to throw him off stride and keep him guessing. But for the heavy duty during the match, all the experts rely on a medium-paced serve with lots of twist to pull the receiver out of court. And as soon as they serve, they charge for the net.

Now, what does the receiver do when he receives this serve? He has three choices: hit down the alley, hit cross-court, or lob.

Take a look at Figure 8, showing the usual position of all four players at the instant the server hits his serve. You'll notice that the server's partner is within about four feet of the center line. This is still close enough to his own backhand alley so that, if he sees the receiver is going to send one straight down the alley, there's usually plenty of time to step over and cut off that attempted alley shot. When he does cut it off, he's in a beautiful position, and his opponents are out of luck. He can dink the ball over with a gentle shot that plops into his opponents' forehand service court—generally for an ace, because the man at the net is too far to the side to reach it, and the man who received service is too far back. Or, if the server's partner doesn't feel like dinking it, he can always volley it cross-court, into his opponents' backhand corner, thereby putting it behind the poor helpless victim at the net for a clean winner.

That's why the receiver seldom tries to return a serve down the line. It's too risky. It leaves his own team wide open if the alley shot isn't an ace.

Instead, the receiver usually angles his return into the server's half of the court so that the server's partner at the net has no chance to volley it. He tries to put it at the feet of the inrushing server. In order to do this, he has to make his drive shallow, not deep. A deep drive would be a juicy target which the server could probably take on the fly. Now do you begin to see why the hard hitter, who specializes in long drives, is at a disadvantage in doubles?

The receiver's other option is to return the serve with a lob. The lob is a dangerous offensive weapon in doubles. It's an efficient way to turn the tables, driving the attackers back from the net and meanwhile giving the

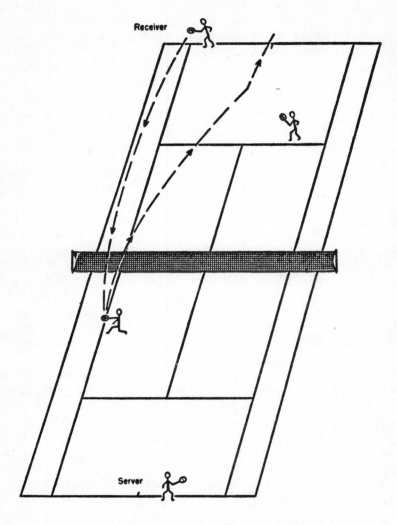

Figure 9. Receiver returns ball down the line.
This facilitates an easy placement for net player.

defenders time to rush the net themselves. However, the lob isn't quite as commonly used for returning service as it is later in the rally. Why? Because the lobber's partner is at the net, instead of in the backcourt. Anything less than a first-class lob will mean that the lobber's partner will lose his front teeth. When a team lobs, both of its members should be in the back court.

Therefore, you don't see a serve returned by lobbing as often as you see it returned with a low cross-court shot. In fact, you'll see the first few plays of every big doubles match follow the same pattern about 80 per cent of the time: Server hits an American twist, breaking wide, and instantly starts for the net. Receiver returns a low shallow drive into the server's half of the court. The server gets to the ball about at the service line, and returns it with a volley or else takes it just after it hits, returning it with a half volley. His shot is an angled one—almost never straight, because that would be playing right into the hands of his opponent waiting directly across the net from him. He angles it either between his two opponents, or more sharply toward their forehand sideline in the hope of pulling the man on that side far out of court.

Up to this time, you'll notice, neither side has tried for a kill. Nobody has hit the ball hard. They're all fencing and jockeying for an opening.

Exactly what kind of opening do they want? They want a rising ball.

Invitation to Murder

Any time you send over a ball that your doubles opponent can take shoulder high, or higher, in his own forecourt, you're simply inviting him to kill it. When a good doubles player is at the net, a rising ball is just what he's waiting and praying for. If he gets it, the point is over.

"Make them hit up" is the theory of net play in doubles. By the same token, "Never hit up" is the cardinal principle of the team that's on the defensive. That's what the rally is all about. It's the attackers at the net, fighting to extract a high ball from the defenders, who in turn are struggling desperately to keep the ball at the attackers' feet and drive them back from the net.

A straight, hard, passing shot isn't tried too often in championship

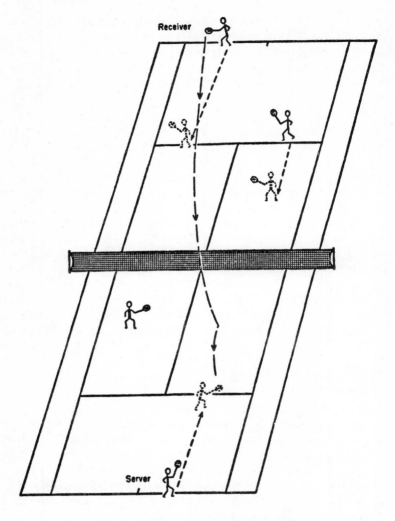

Figure 10. Receiver returns with a low, shallow
drive into server's half of the court—with all four
players moving into position.

doubles. Both members of a team always take the net together, and once they get there it's a tough job to pass them. What a difference from singles! If you take the net in singles, your opponent will try to blaze the ball past you, because there's plenty of empty space on each side of you. But there isn't much room left for passing when two men divide the net between them. They can usually cut off the fastest ball without jumping too far.

This is the real reason that there are so few sizzling drives in doubles. A hard drive is always rising as it travels through the forecourt. And with two men waiting for it in the forecourt, that rising ball is going to be massacred. Its speed merely makes it go back faster when the net player shoves his racket in front of it. All the net man has to do is block it off, angling it to the side, and it's gone.

Therefore, the typical shot in modern doubles is a low, rather soft cross-court shot. Soft because it should just clear the net and then start dropping—not continue rising so the other team gets a downward shot at it. Low because the other team will then have to dig it out of the dirt, and perhaps hit it upward high enough to be killed. Cross-court because a doubles court is wider than singles, leaving a wider margin for error; because a slanting shot doesn't reach the net so soon, and therefore doesn't have to rise so steeply; because a ball to the side pulls a man out of position.

How to Drive Them Back

A service break is a great victory in doubles. One break generally is enough to win the set because every good team holds its serve consistently. It's no uncommon thing for a set to go fourteen or sixteen games, in tournament doubles, before one team cracks the other's service. The reason is that the serving team has a bigger advantage in doubles than in singles. In doubles, the servers are always at the net before the receivers get their first chance to hit the ball.

Therefore, the team that receives service is in hot water immediately. It's on the defensive. If it makes a false move, if it gives the attackers a ball high enough to smash (or even to volley down), the point is probably over.

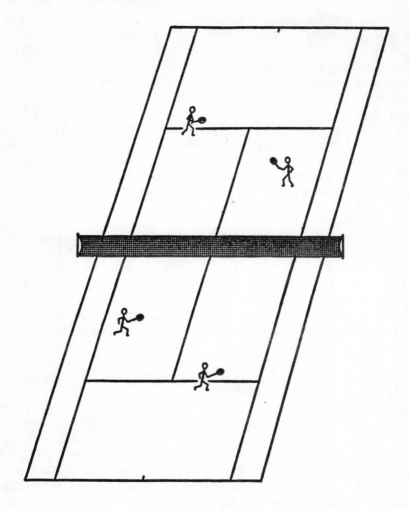

Figure 11. Winning doubles necessitates all four
players at net often—waiting for the all-impor-
tant rising ball that they can volley away for a
placement.

The big question, for the defenders, always is, how can we drive them back from the net?

There are two ways to do it. One way is to hit to their feet. The other is to lob to their baseline.

Neither is easy. But the first is harder than the second. It takes finesse to stroke a ball delicately enough so that it clears the net and then drops at the feet of a man in forecourt. George Lott, who many experts think was the greatest doubles player in history, had a "dink" shot that was one of his most dangerous weapons. Bobby Riggs, Okker, Ashe, and Nastase are other masters of this type of shallow, fast-dropping shot. Whenever a good player hits a ball that he knows will drop at an opponent's feet, he and his partner both storm the net at once so they can get close enough to kill the rising ball which they know the opponent must return. That's how it happens that you sometimes see all four players in forecourt, fencing with each other, struggling to make the enemy hit up or at least retreat into the backcourt.

A lob always forces an opponent to retreat. Obviously he has to run back in order to retrieve the ball. However, several things can go wrong with a lob.

It may be too shallow. When this happens, the enemy can stay inside the service line, hit it on the fly without waiting for it to bounce, and usually put it away. A lob is hard to place just right—it has to arch high enough so that it's over the net man's head and can't be smashed, yet it also has to drop steeply enough so that it won't sail out of court before it lands. A nice problem in trajectories!

Most star players kill a lob if they can stay near or inside the service line to hit it. If they have to back up farther, they don't try to put it away because they know that the opposition has enough time to retrieve it no matter where they hit. Instead they try to hit deep and rush forward again while the ball is still traveling toward their opponents. Unless a man sees that his partner is having trouble handling the lob, he'll even stay up there at the net and wait for his partner to return to forecourt after hitting it.

Naturally there's a lot of surging back and forth, advancing and retreating, in doubles as it's played among the higher echelons. There's a lightninglike exchange at the net, and finally a reverberating smash. That's big-time doubles.

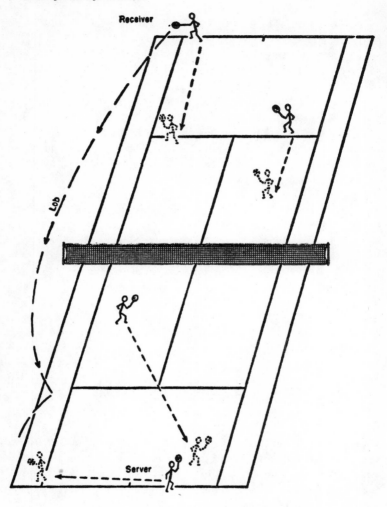

Figure 12. Receiver lobs over opponent at net.
Server moves left to cover lob. Server's partner
retreats diagonally. Receiving team advances
immediately to net.

In small-time doubles, the general idea is the same—to get the net and make your opponents hit upward to you—but the maneuvers are likely to be different. Starting with the next chapter, we'll go into the tactics that should enable you to plaster your pals in a friendly doubles game at the club or public courts.

11 / Middle-Class Doubles

You're a middle-class player if you have reasonably good strokes, some brains, and enough zing in your legs to rush the net or chase a lob. You belong to the upper crust only if you travel the grass-court circuit from tournament to tournament, or at least rate a seeding in the biggest tourney in your part of the country. Contrariwise, you're in the tennis proletariat when you're too slow to go into the forecourt, or too awkward to get your racket on a ball below your shoulders.

If you're in the tennis aristocracy, among the "amateur" stars who devote their whole life to the game, this chapter isn't for you. Better go back and read Chapter 10 again while the rest of the audience is attending to this one.

If you're definitely low-class on a court, give this chapter a light once-over, just as you did the previous one. You'll need it for background. We'll get to you in later pages, but you'll understand them better if you've read these earlier ones. After all, you'll never improve your aim unless you have a target to shoot at. Maybe you haven't the time or ability to play middle-class tennis, but your own game will be sounder if you know how the game *should* be played.

And now for the rest of you—the suffering, swearing devotees who rush to the tennis club or the park courts on Saturdays and Sundays, who may enter one or two local tournaments a year, who play fairly well but keep tearing out handfuls of hair because you don't play better—this is your introduction to the vast subject of your own doubles game and how to improve it. Middle-class doubles is a pastime of limitless possibilities for fun and exercise. You'll get more of both as you wise up.

One Up, or Two?

There are two common styles of play in middle-class doubles. In the West, where even the older players are on the courts all year around and stay in fairly good shape, it's usual for both players to go to the net together. Most western players see a lot of tournament tennis since there are so many tournaments going on out there all the time. They're pretty thoroughly imbued with the offensive style of play since they keep seeing it in tournaments. And they're also hep on to the fact that anyone who uses his head can get to the net without running. (More about that later.) This is why, on Pacific Coast courts, you usually see both members of one team or the other at the net.

The picture is different in the rest of the country. The one-up-and-one-back formation is common there. Even among men who once were good enough for intercollegiate competition, only one player at a time will rush the net. This is partly because the climate keeps them off the courts for months at a time, which means that they're likely to tire more easily when tennis season does come around. And it's partly because the East is more conservative and hasn't yet been sold on the headlong, attacking style of play the westerners like.

I think if you once try the two-up style you'll like it, and you'll find it doesn't take such strong legs as you'd think. However, just in case you're partial to the school of thought that advocates only one man going to the net, let's talk about that style of play first.

If you're using this one-up, one-back style, the man at the net usually should station himself on the backhand side, while his partner stays at the baseline on the forehand side. If the net man darts across to cut off a ball far to his right, the rear man naturally moves leftward to cover him.

If you're playing net while your partner serves, be ready to fall back a bit if you see it's a weak serve. On the other hand, when it's a strong serve, crowd in close so you can really climb aboard the return and finish the point pronto.

This formation is primarily a defensive formation. So don't try to attack until you see a gaping hole. Both of you should stay back quite a bit. Keep getting the ball back, smoothly and carefully, always aiming for the center where you can't miss. Lob a lot. Let the other fellows do the running and the smashing and the gambling. Let them try to nick the lines for aces. They'll make the errors and you'll win the points. The only time you should hit a hard drive, or a hard volley, is when you think you can win the point with that shot.

The net man should keep sliding forward and back in his half of the court—racing in when his partner makes a good shot, retreating when he makes a weak one. The baseline man can do some sliding forward and back too. If a short drive comes to him, he ought to move in to meet it, and perhaps follow his shot to the net if that looks feasible.

Mostly, however, he'll be moving from side to side as his partner cuts over to volley, or as his opponents lob over the net man's head. Clever opponents can make the lone baseline man run himself crazy if they keep lobbing to one corner and then the other. When you run into these cute tactics, just pull the net man back whenever necessary, so that both of you are on the baseline to defend against lobs and drives.

The western style of doubles, which is closer to the style you see in tournament tennis, involves keeping both men back together, then both going up together. When both men are at the net they're mighty hard to dislodge. The two-up tactics were covered pretty well in the last chapter.

However, middle-class players make mistakes which topflight players don't make, regardless of the formation they use. Whether you play one-up or two-up, there are some common sins of commission and omission that you'd better guard against.

Sins of the Server

Doubles, as I reminded you in the last chapter, is more a matter of intelligence than of muscle and speed. A player may have the constitution of a commando and the strokes of a Kramer, but if he isn't hep on to doubles strategy he'll be nothing but a stumblebum when he goes up against a pair of smart middle-class players. Unfortunately, most middle-class players aren't as smart as they should be. They may be double-domed deep thinkers in industry or art, but for some reason they don't analyze the problems of outmaneuvering two guys on the other side of a net. They just whale the ball until they're arm weary, and run till they drop. At the club where I'm pro, lots of members earn big salaries in movies or business, but some of them would be making about $25 a week if they showed the same amount of brains in their work that they show while they're bounding around a tennis court.

Let's analyze the common mistakes made in middle-class doubles. We'll begin with the server. His first blunder, of course, is that he hits his first serve too hard. Chapter 10 showed you why the top doubles players take it easy when they serve: they want to get to the net, which can't be done with a blazing service because it comes back too soon.

The second blunder is in hitting the second serve too gently. It's the same sad story as in middle-class singles: a thundering first serve that is faulted, then a patball second serve that the receiver eats up. This sickly second ball is even more disastrous in doubles, however, because it lets the receivers grab the net position immediately if they want it. Instead of being on the offensive as they always should be in a service game, the server and his helpless partner are backed up against the baseline, facing two bloodthirsty volleyers just across the net.

So if you want your partner to like you, develop a smooth, reliable, medium-paced second serve. However, you'll never be really popular as long as you have to serve twice to get the ball in. A doubles player who usually misses his first serve isn't a real player at all. He's a drag on his partner and a drug on the market.

That first serve is enormously important in doubles. Most players have no idea how important it is, nor why. Just think about all these factors:

The psychological difference alone will pay off in points. If your opponents see that your first serve is spectacular but ineffective, they'll gain a lot of confidence. They don't have to worry about your serve. They can relax while the first one goes into the net, then close in to hit a good lick at the second. On the other hand, if your first serve keeps clicking, they're in trouble. They're frustrated. They keep wishing for a chance at the juicy second serve, and they don't get it. Nobody feels happy when he's facing a server who never misses.

This psychology makes a difference in court position, too. Invariably, in both topflight and middle-class doubles, the receivers move in a step or two for the second serve. That always means trouble for the servers. It means the return of service will come at them sooner. It means they'll have more difficulty in holding the net position. Therefore, even if the second serve is a good one, the server's team is almost always in hot water from the start. You want to keep your receiver back, and the best way to do that is to make him start play from the first-serve position.

And then there's the matter of the wear and tear on your own muscles. In a long match, if you're regularly hitting two serves instead of one to get the ball into play, you'll feel a definite difference in the last set. This is even more serious in doubles than singles. A doubles server moves forward the instant he serves, particularly if he's playing the western style. Now, if you take about four steps before you see that the ball is a fault, and then walk four steps back to the baseline to try again, that's eight steps you've wasted on one serve. Therefore, if you generally miss your first serve, you travel about the equivalent of a city block, half-running and half-walking, in one or two service games. When you've added those extra blocks to the mileage you cover in a tough match, the depreciation and obsolescence and general subtraction from your resources just can't be ignored.

Which brings us to another common mistake in middle-class doubles teams who try to play the two-up formation. Maybe you wait to see whether or not your serve goes in. In that case, you're saving stamina—but you're losing points. A fraction of a second looms large when you're trying to get into position to handle a return of service. That fraction of a second means a couple of yards. Then why, in the name of sanity, do so many club players stand on the baseline after they've served, craning their neck to see whether the serve is good, and finally, a full second or more behind time, start their rush after the ball has already bounced?

It's sheer stupidity. If your opponent makes a decent return of your serve, you can't possibly get to the service line fast enough to volley it or half volley it unless you've started forward in the same motion as you served. Don't wait! Get going! As you finish serving and your right shoulder and right hip move across the baseline in your follow-through, just let that motion flow into the first stride of your dash to the net. Cultivate a serve-and-run sequence that is all one continuous movement. You can watch the flight of your serve as you run forward. Players who run while they watch, instead of standing still to watch, always have an advantage.

Another sad shortcoming of many middle-class servers is that they

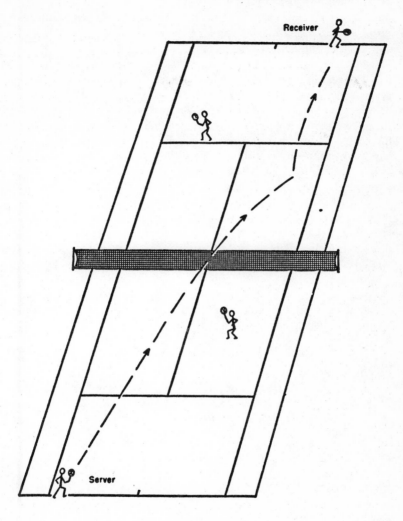

Figure 13. Server moves toward own alley to
serve when having trouble placing the ball to
opponent's backhand.

don't know where to serve from. They stand near the center line, as they do in singles—instead of moving far over to the side, which usually is the strategic thing to do in doubles.

When you're serving from your backhand side, move to the extreme left. Get within a few feet of your backhand alley. Then serve diagonally across toward your receiver's backhand corner. It's easier to snipe at his corner when you have this better angle because you have a bigger margin for error. And he'll be pulled farther off the court to make a return with his backhand, which is presumably his weakest stroke. (In case you're in any doubt as to why you shouldn't try this same attractive serving angle in singles, just reflect on what can happen if you don't have a partner covering the forehand half of your court. If the receiver just pokes the ball back somehow, into that big unguarded territory, you're dead.)

When you're serving from your forehand side, it's usually a good idea to give your receiver another wide-angle serve that takes him across his forehand sideline. The wider the better. This means, of course, that you'll serve from only a few feet inside your own forehand sideline.

However, this isn't always smart. It depends on your opponent. Maybe he has a terrific forehand. Or maybe he's so fleet-footed that it does you no good to make him run out of court; he always gets back in time. Or maybe his backhand is so atrocious that you ought to hammer at it incessantly.

In any of these cases, your strategy should be to place the ball on his backhand, no matter which side you serve from. How can you do this when you're serving from your forehand side? Just stand at the center line. Then send your serve almost straight down the center, with only enough angle so that it slants into the backhand corner of his forehand service court. Look at Figure 14 and you'll see what I mean.

Sins of the Receivers

The receiving team makes plenty of mistakes too. One mistake, as you probably realize by now, is in trying to belt the return of service too hard. This is silly, against a server who comes in to volley as soon as he has served. It's silly even if the server stays back and there's only one man at the net. A hard-hit ball is just what the net man wants. It will still be waist high, or higher, as it passes over the service line—and that's where he's going to meet it. All he has to do is put his racket in front of it. Its own speed will make it rebound fast enough to clear the net, and if he angles it to the side or down at an opponent's feet, the point is over.

Another mistake is in standing in the wrong spot to receive service. The average player always stands in the same place against all servers. You ought to study the server, see how deep his serve usually goes and where he aims it, then figure out where to take it. There isn't too much variation in an ordinary player's serves. He'll almost always put them in approximately the same part of the service court. Same depth, same speed, same angle. This makes it possible for you to scout him, in his first few service games, and set yourself for him thereafter.

But remember that no two players are alike. For every server you face you'll stand in a different spot, if you use your eyes and your head. Break yourself of the habit of taking up a stance at the same old spot, no matter who's serving.

The chances are, you're standing too far back, against everybody you meet. Remember, this isn't singles. You're not supposed to return service with a drive to the baseline. You're supposed to send back a low, shallow ball—which means a soft ball, not a hard-hit one. You can usually manage this just by putting your racket on it with very little backswing. All right, figure it out. If you were going to drive, naturally you'd need more time to get set, so you'd stand farther back to take the serve. But since you're not going to need so much time to draw your racket back, why not stand in closer and take the ball on the rise? Maybe you'll have to practice a while before you can do this for backhand returns, but for a forehand shot it will be easier than you think. The sooner you send that serve back, the less time there'll be for the opposition to get close enough to volley it. Even if you just pop the ball back, when you do it from close range you're likely to give him a low-bouncing ball that he'll have to hit up to you. So move in, as much as a foot inside the baseline, and get your racket on that serve fast!

This goes double when you're waiting for the second serve. You probably move up closer for it, but not close enough. Even in big-time doubles, against the best servers in the game, smart receivers get three or

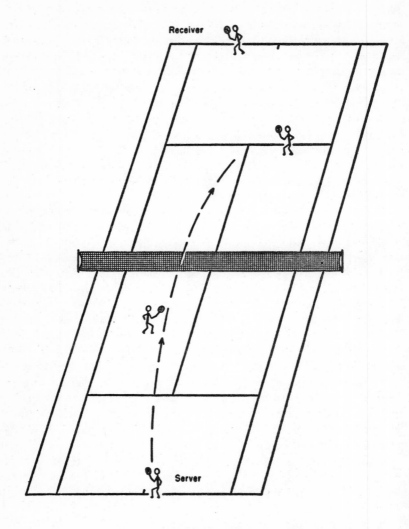

Figure 14. When serving from forehand side,
server stands near center line to serve.

four feet inside the baseline. In middle-class doubles, where the server's second ball is usually a sitting duck, the receiver ought to be still farther inside the baseline. You'll feel as if you're in the cannon's mouth, the first few times you stand that close, and you'll probably be hurried in returning the serve. That's all right. Handle it awkwardly if you must. Just poke it back. As you see what trouble it gives your opponents when you poke it into the half of the court covered by the server, you'll feel better.

Don Budge could receive any serve in doubles without moving more than one step. Why? Because he stood so close. When an opposing server tried to pull him out of court with a wide-angled serve to the corner, Don was so close to the corner itself that he could cut it off before it had time to bounce very far to the side. Remember this when you go up against a smart server who starts running you out of court with wide serves. Move up close and cut him off fast, especially when he's on your forehand. Keep your eye on the ball from the instant it leaves his racket, and you won't have too much trouble taking that one step in time to meet it.

Another thing that saddens me, whenever I watch a doubles match at the club, is that I almost never see a lob used to return service. A lob is poison in middle-class tennis, but almost nobody seems to realize this. If you ever watch high-grade doubles you see lobs constantly—yet how many do you see on the public courts or in the tennis clubs?

Topflight players lob in the middle of rallies more frequently than they do in returning service. I explained why in the last chapter. But those reasons don't apply in middle-class tennis. You'll get good results by returning a serve with a lob every few points. The threat of the lob, as much as the lob itself, is a weapon. It will keep your opponents on pins and needles. They won't dare move in to the net as close as they'd like to. And they'll never be sure whether they're going to be volleying or chasing a high ball back to the baseline.

Any time a serve comes at you that's really hard to handle, try lobbing. The only alternative is to make a weak return which the man at the net can assassinate. Your lob will make your opponent run back—and don't forget that you want to keep him running, so he'll tire sooner. Maybe he'll get to it fast enough so that he can smash. You still haven't lost the point. Most middle-class doubles players have a surprisingly erratic overhead. The smash may hit the back fence or the bottom of the net. If it lands in court, you or your partner can retrieve it most of the time. Anybody smashing from the back court isn't likely to put the ball away. He has to beat two men, and the ball has to travel yards and yards before it's dead. The only time a well-placed smash is a sure winner is when it's hit from well inside the service line—and if your lob is even half good, when you use it to return service you'll place the ball far enough back to prevent the other team from taking it in the forecourt.

Keep lobbing, whether you're returning service or fighting your way through a long rally. Sure, the other team will smash your lobs. But they'll miss, more than half the time. And they'll be getting arm weary and leg weary from all the running and smashing. And whenever you place a lob deep enough, you may extract a return that gives you a chance to come up to the net.

Stop Being Statuesque

When the ball is hit to your partner, do you stand like a statue and wait for something to happen in your territory? Most middle-class doubles players do. But they shouldn't.

It's a sign of an unsophisticated player, this business of being rooted to the ground when the ball is in your partner's section of the court. An astute doubles player is constantly on the move, forward or back, to one side or the other, depending on where the ball goes. Let's consider the strategy that dictates his movements.

Suppose your opponents are serving, and your partner is receiving. (See Figure 15.) Before the serve, you'll take a stance just inside the service line. But don't become a statue. Watch the serve, and decide whether it's going to be tough or easy for your partner to handle. Watch what your partner does with it. If his return is very good, then you should be moving in because your opponents are probably going to have to hit the ball upward, and you'll want to pounce on it at the net. On the other hand, if the serve is a tricky one and your partner is hard-pressed to get it back, then his ball will be rising—and your opponents will be doing the pouncing. So where should you be? Obviously, in the back court, on the defensive, ready to retrieve that volley from your opponents. If you stay up close, you may lose your front teeth.

Suppose your partner decides to return the serve by lobbing. If it's a really deep lob that your opponents have to chase far beyond the baseline, you (and your partner, if he's playing western style) will both want to come to the net to cut off the return. But if it's just an average lob, you'd better back up. The smash is likely to pass you before you can touch it, if you're in the forecourt.

Take another situation. You're the server's partner this time. Let's assume he'll be charging in as soon as he's served. He'll need the maximum protection down the center because he has to cover his own outside line. Therefore, you ought to be in the center of the service court, about halfway between the net and the service line. Most players keep edging over toward their own alley. They keep thinking about that big open space on the outside. They don't realize that the ball is almost never going down that alley. It's too hard a shot to try. Almost anybody can see it coming in time to step across and block it off.

Furthermore, if you hang around near the alley, you're leaving two alternatives open to the man who receives your partner's serve. He can smack the ball right down the center, and probably pass both of you. Or else he can make a wide cross-court shot and put the ball behind your partner. Both these shots are easy for the receiver if you leave him the opening. So quit worrying about the outside so much and edge over to cover the inside.

Suppose the receiver decides to lob over your head. The question instantly arises, who should cover it? You or your partner? There should be an understanding about this before the match starts. You and your teammate may work out some agreement about signals, or calling for the ball, or giving every doubtful lob to the man who is the harder smasher. Anyhow, let's assume that your partner is going to take this lob. Then what should you do? Just stand serenely where you are, and wait to see what happens? That's what the dumb players do. The smart ones are moving as soon as that lob starts to climb through the air.

Play it smart. Your partner is crossing over behind you to take the lob. Why stay on the same side of the court as he is? You're leaving the other side completely unpopulated. Get over there. It's up to you to trade sides with your partner, instead of trusting that he'll rush back again to cover

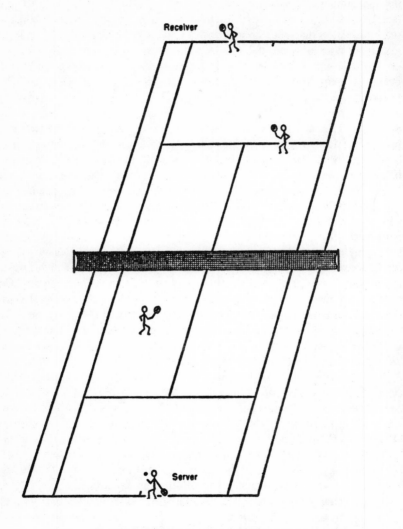

Figure 15. Receiver's partner stands just inside
the service line.

his own side after retrieving the lob. If the lob is a fairly shallow one, and you see he's going to slam it back for a possible winner, then your team should stay on the offensive. So where should you be? Up at the net, of course. While he crosses over to get the lob, you should be crossing over to cover the other half of the net. Then he'll move straight forward, after hitting the ball, to cover his own half of the net.

On the other hand, if the lob is a beautiful deep one that may land inches inside the baseline, or if your partner is bothered by sun in his eyes, or wind, or any other difficulty—then you'd better get out of the forecourt fast. Your team has lost the offensive, and the place for you is back beside your partner at the baseline. Cross over diagonally, heading for the corner he was occupying before the lob was hit. If this sounds complicated, just look at Figure 12 and I think you'll get the idea.

Now let's suppose that your partner has just served, and the receiver is about to hit it back. Don't stand still. You should be moving. Where? Anywhere, just a little. I mean that you should appear to be moving, more than you actually are. You want to keep the receiver guessing. Your continuous moving will have a tendency to push the return over toward the server; if the receiver isn't sure whether you're far over toward your own alley or far over toward the center, he'll probably play a cross-court shot to be sure of keeping the ball away from you. And of course this is exactly what you want. As your partner comes in to the net after serving, a cross-court return will give him a chance to make a forehand volley—which he probably prefers to a backhand volley.

This little strategy of feinting is always good in doubles. Use it constantly. Keep up the appearance of moving, so that the other side is never sure exactly where you are. Whenever you're charging up to the net from backcourt, try to look as if you're heading where you aren't. Whenever you're standing still waiting for the opposition to return the ball, keep swaying, and pretending to start this way or that. The hardest man to beat is a man whose whereabouts you don't know.

However, when your team is at the net in western-style doubles, there's always a definite place where you should be for every shot: you should be halving the territory through which the shot can possibly be returned. Look at Figure 16. There's only a certain segment of the net over which the ball can be returned, and still have a chance of dropping inside the court. Therefore you should ignore the rest of the net. Why cover it? Just cover the part where the ball may come. You and your partner should divide up that part of the net, each of you taking half. If you're playing eastern style, whichever man is at the net should move into the center of the "angle of return," just as he would in singles.

This means that you will be constantly shifting, moving to one side or the other depending on where you've sent the ball. If you've volleyed to the right, you move over to the right. If it's really a wide shot, the left-hand partner will move almost to the center line. Any return to his left has a very small opening and is almost sure to go out.

Likewise, when you volley to the left, a net man should move to the left. And when you volley down the center, both members should close up on the center. It's amazing how few club players understand this. When the ball isn't in their territory they just stand, dumb and happy, wherever they happen to be. And then they curse because the return shot catches them out of position. They just don't play the angles.

Patience Pays Off

Most doubles players are too impetuous. They lose points by trying for a kill too soon. And they wear themselves down by hitting harder than they need to.

When you take the net, play cat-and-mouse. Never hurry the kill. Instead, force it to arrive inevitably by putting the other team more and more on the defensive until they hand you the point on a platter. The strategy of net play is to force the defenders gradually into such a hot spot that they can make only an easy return. Then you can volley for an ace without even hitting hard.

If you're ready to put the ball away, and you have the whole court, why hit it with all your strength? The only time you need to hit hard at the net is when you're shooting for a small opening. If the other team has given you an opening big enough to fly an airplane through, relax and tap the ball away gently. It saves your strength, and it makes the other team feel silly, to see you acing them without even trying hard.

It's a common mistake for the server to rush in and try to put the ball

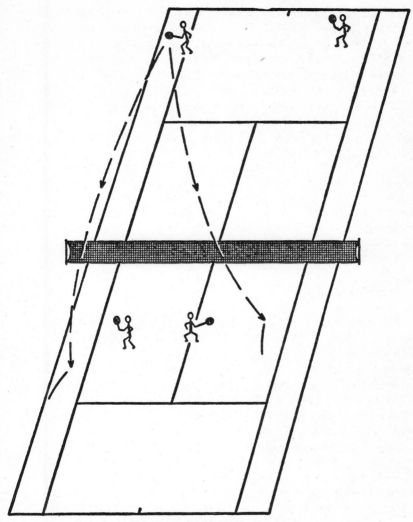

Figure 16. Net players divide only that part of
the court in which the ball can possibly be
returned.

away with his first volley. This almost never works. In fact, it usually gets the server into bad trouble. His attempted ace is cut off by the man across the net from him, and immediately the server's team is on the defensive if it hasn't lost the point outright.

When you're serving, be patient. Of course, in two-up tennis you should start forward like a satellite as soon as you hit your serve, but you should slow down as you near the service line so you'll have better balance for your volley. Don't try to ace it unless the ball is high and you're a powerful hitter. If it's below the net as you hit it, or if it's on your backhand or somewhere else that's one of your weaknesses, don't try an angle shot to the sideline. Just put it diagonally across into the opposition's forehand service court so their man waiting at the net in the backhand court can't get to it. Then, as soon as you've hit, move in farther! This is another shortcoming of most middle-class players. After hitting their first volley from about the service line, they stand and wait to see where it goes.

The closer to the net you get, the better, as long as the opposition doesn't lob. If you're sure a lob isn't coming, just keep crowding the net and wait for your chance to put the ball away. While the defense keeps getting the ball back well, your strategy is to keep volleying to the center, or better still a little off center, so that the man on their forehand side has to take the ball on his backhand. Keep your volleys as deep as possible, and soft enough so they don't bounce high. Whenever you're in doubt about where to put the ball, simply send it at the feet of one of your opponents. When you finally get a weak return, step in and kill it with a shot to the sideline.

Of all the faults of middle-class doubles players, the biggest and commonest fault is in trying to put the ball away too often. Play it safe, and you'll play better.

12 / Ghost Doubles: A New Kind of Practice Game

When Singles Get Too Strenuous

Once past the peak of tournament condition, few people play singles for fun. They've learned that doubles is more sociable, more interesting, less tiring. That's why you almost invariably see foursomes rather than twosomes on club courts. Even the great world-class professionals, when they foregather to have a little fun, get up four-handed games rather than singles.

Therefore if you've played mostly singles so far, you ought to be looking ahead. The day will come when your usual "friendly" singles session will become too strenuous for you. And then you may suddenly find that you've become a social wallflower at the tennis club. People don't like to play doubles with someone who is known as primarily a singles player. They've learned that a hotshot singles winner is likely to be a misfit on a doubles team.

Why? Because a pair who know anything about doubles tactics will simply move in close and murder him, or sit back and lob him to death. His thunderbolt serve and flat hard drives are almost useless because they come back to him too fast, before he can reach the net. His habit of racing all over the court causes collisions with his partner. He's caught out of position time after time or falls over his own feet, because he doesn't know where his opponents are likely to put the ball. So the doubles players consider him a flat tire despite his sledgehammer strokes and his speed afoot. While the rest of the gang plays doubles, he's as uninvolved as a skier in the Sahara.

But he needn't be.

If he has just one friend, he can improve his doubles techniques without actually playing doubles. He can get the practice he needs by playing "ghost doubles."

Doubles on the Half Court

You don't really need three other people in order to practice doubles. You and your pal can do it all by yourselves. Instead of playing singles you can play what I call ghost doubles, and probably have more fun than you would at singles. Here's how.

You and your sparring partner simply agree that two quarters of the tennis court are out-of-bounds.

Those quarters (the shaded sections in Figures 17 and 18) will be the sections that your nonexistent ghost partners would cover in a conventional doubles game.

Thus when you serve from the forehand (right-hand) side of the court, your backhand side is just a black hole in space, and so is your opponent's. And on the next point, when you move over to serve from the left side, each player's right side (forehand half of the court) then becomes taboo. Consequently all shots must be aimed cross-court—just as they are most of the time in regular doubles.

Do you see the logic of this? Look at the diagrams, and think a moment. Or review the strategy of doubles explained in the two previous chapters.

Diagonal Is the Only Way to Go

Figure 8 shows the usual positions of all four players in a doubles game at the instant the server hits his serve. If the receiver is silly enough to return it down the line or thereabouts, the server's partner at the net can easily step over and cut it off for a sure point. That's why the receiver in doubles almost invariably angles his return into the server's half of the court, to keep it out of the reach of the server's partner in the other half. This is true whether the server is starting play on the right-hand or left-hand half of the court.

Now what does the server normally do when his service is hit back toward him? He also angles it cross-court. If he were to hit it straight, the receiver's partner in the forecourt could volley it out of reach. All this adds up to the fact that two of the four players in a doubles match are out of the action a good part of the time.

Therefore in ghost doubles you simply agree that a ball hit into the ghost's half of the court (the shaded section) is a lost point for the player who hits it. This means that the two nonghostly players must keep hitting cross-court—as they usually would in an actual doubles game.

Single Players but Doubles Tactics

You'll find that ghost doubles is a game where you and your lone opponent play doubles-style, using doubles-type strokes and tactics.

You'll lob, dink, and perhaps volley more than you could in singles. After your serve you'll probably move straight ahead toward the net— remembering that you have only half of it to guard.

Likewise, since you want as much time as possible to get up into the forecourt, your serve will probably be the one normally used in doubles: the kind which arches about head-high over the net and kicks wide to the side when it lands.

Whether you're serving or receiving, your objective in ghost doubles will be the same as in normal doubles: to work your way toward the net in the half of the court from which you served or received, and then to make your opponent give you a rising ball that you can smack down at his feet or past him into the alley. Of course, the alley is considered in-bounds in ghost doubles—on the nonghost or unshaded half of each court, that is.

You can play three sets of vigorous ghost doubles without getting any more tired than you would in one set of singles. Moreover, you'll get twice as much doubles-style practice as you would in conventional doubles— because you'll serve every second game instead of every fourth; you'll receive all your opponent's serves instead of half of them; and he'll hit all balls toward your half of the court. Obviously you'll do a lot more hitting, and a lot less standing around, than you would in doubles. Likewise you'll do much less chugging around the court than a singles player does.

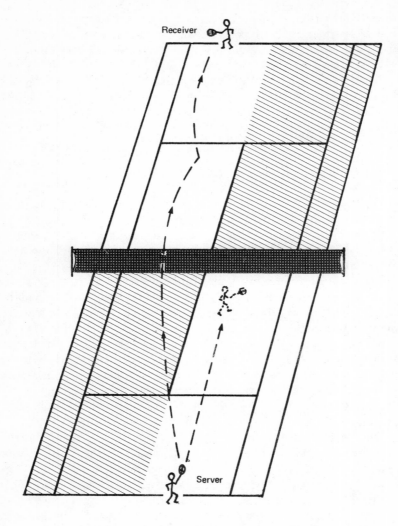

Figure 17. Ghost doubles. In this game only
cross-court shots are allowed.

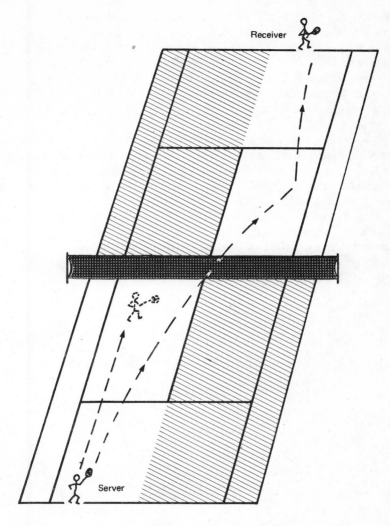

Figure 18. Ghost doubles. Server sends
a serve as usual to receiver's left.

It's as if you and your opponent each had a perfect doubles partner who covers his own part of the court like a security blanket, never poaches on his teammate's sector, never growls or glares, never gets in the way. What could be more peaceful than playing doubles without a partner to plague you?

Around 1964 I hit on this idea as a teaching device to help a pupil practice the basic strokes and tactics of doubles. At first we just rallied cross-court, but rallying isn't as much fun as keeping score, so we made a game out of it.

It worked so well that I now play it with many of my pupils. They find it not only brings quick improvement in their doubles game but helps their singles game too, if that's what they want—because when the play is kept in this smaller area they can concentrate on whichever strokes they want to improve, without racing all over court to get in position.

As indicated in the beginning, ghost doubles practice can do a lot to make you a popular doubles partner. Whether age twenty or sixty, a crafty doubles player is always in demand. So the next time you and a friend have a court to yourselves, instead of playing singles you might try ghost doubles. I'll bet you like it.

13 / Outsmart Them

Always Change a Losing Game

Woe is you. Woe is your partner. You're taking a beating.

You clench your teeth and fight like fury. You give each other pep talks. You run and jump and flail the air, giving each ball the old college try. But it doesn't seem to do much good. You're still making too many errors, and the enemy is still making too many aces. What to do?

Get crafty. Get devious.

Brains are one of the rarest of all commodities in middle-class doubles. If you and your partner will only use your head, and start plotting instead of just struggling, you'll get Old Man Statistics on your side. You'll become one of those remarkably rare teams which think. That in itself will probably win for you. An intelligent team almost always whips a dumb one.

The first question to consider is this: What change should you make in your style of play?

Obviously you need a change. A drastic change. If you keep on playing as you have, your opponents will keep on playing as *they* have. Barring an unlucky streak on the other side of the net, or a sudden rainstorm, the match will soon be over and your score will be on the wrong side of the hyphen.

Fighting harder isn't the answer. To turn the tables, you need to make your opponents play differently. The way to make them is to play differently yourself.

All right, make an analysis. How are they beating you? What are they doing that's so hard to handle?

If They're Tough at the Net

Maybe they're coming to the net and you can't dislodge them. They're sharp volleyers. They're firing your balls into the corners for aces.

Don't despair. There are several answers to a strong net game. Especially in middle-class doubles. Every middle-class team has plenty of weaknesses. Let's start probing.

You have several choices. You can: (a) give them balls that are harder to volley; (b) storm the net yourselves, even though they're already up there, and fight it out with them at point-blank range; (c) get to the net before they do, and force them to stay back; (d) start an intensive lobbing campaign.

Let's take these alternatives in the order named.

They may be good volleyers, but they can't be equally good on both sides, and at all heights and angles. Which member of the team is the weaker volleyer? Make him do all the volleying. Which is his weaker side? Probably the backhand. Then keep all the balls on his backhand (or his forehand, in the rare cases where he prefers to volley off his port side). Don't be content just to feed them to that general area, either. Make him hit from the angles he dislikes. For most players, a high backhand volley is one of their weakest shots. Try him out on those. He'll probably hate them. Try him out on low backhand volleys whenever you can. He may have so much trouble picking them up that he'll give you a fine chance to move in for a down volley on his return. The main thing to remember is that a waist-high to head-high ball is the easiest to volley. When you're working on a net player's backhand, make him jump for the ball, or else make him dig it out of the dirt.

Even if the enemy is entrenched at the net, there's no law saying you can't go up there too. It happens every minute in big-time doubles. It should happen oftener in your league. A pair of good volleyers sometimes will get badly rattled when the other team moves in instead of hanging back.

If you want to force the fight in the forecourt, one good way to get up close is to send in a low, slow, shallow cross-court ball and race in behind it. It should be slow, because that gives you more time to get into position. It should be cross-court for the same reason: a diagonal ball takes longer to reach the net than a straight one does. It should be low and shallow if possible because that's the kind of ball that nobody can kill, or even volley down; the return will be a rising ball, unless your opponent has unusual finesse, and a rising ball is just what the doctor ordered for you. Hammer it down at your weaker rival's feet.

Once all four of you are up close, banging away at each other, there'll be less time to think. Everybody has to move like a flash just to cut off the ball, and probably considers himself lucky if he gets it back over the net. Nevertheless, a smart player has an edge over a nonthinker in this way: the smarty decides ahead of time what he'll try to do. Then, when the ball comes smoking in, he may be ready with an answer. Even though there's no time to decide where to return it, he has an edge because he's decided in advance to look for a certain opening and shoot for it if he can.

Make up your mind before you start each exchange in the forecourt where you're going to try to send every ball that comes at you. Probably it will be to the backhand of whichever opponent is the clumsier. Certainly it will be toward somebody's feet. One rising ball now, one smash, and the point is over. I trust you've learned by this time, after all I've said about the subject in previous chapters, that the key to success at the net is in keeping your ball low and extracting a high one from your opposition.

One other weapon you might try, when you're carrying the fight to the enemy at the net, is the lob-volley. It's not easy. But it's devastating when you can control it. Decide in advance, when you're moving up to point-blank range, that as soon as possible you'll try lofting one over their heads. Then grab the first opportunity, and see what happens. At any rate, it will throw them off stride, and even if they can jump high enough to smash it, they may be startled enough to ruin the shot. If you do succeed in getting it too high to reach, and it lands inside the baseline, it's practically a sure winner. More than that, it's an unpleasant surprise to the other team. After a few lob-volleys, they'll never know what to expect from you. Get 'em guessing and they're half beaten.

We'll go into the mechanics of hitting a lob-volley, as well as the other special strokes you need for doubles, in a later chapter. Meanwhile, let's consider how to beat the other team in the race for the net.

When your side is serving, there should be no problem. You already have one man up there. His partner should serve and go in, before the first ball comes back. When you're receiving, it's harder. You can do it, though, if you're playing against ordinary opposition.

The way to do it is to stand closer to receive the serve. Whack it back before the server has time to close in. Try to put it at his feet, in that no-man's land between the service line and the baseline. Then jump into the forecourt, your partner beside you. Keep volleying deep to the center while you fence for an opening to put the ball away. But keep your hair on. Don't hurry too much. Wait until the opening is really big before you try for an ace. You've got the offensive now. Don't lose it by being hasty. Let the other guys do the worrying. Let them make the errors. Just keep pushing the ball back at their feet, and pretty soon something will crack.

Any one of these strategies, or several of them in combination, will probably bollix up a team of net-rushers and throw them badly off their game. However, lobbing is the best strategy of all against a net game.

Some club players seem to have the idea that it's sissy to lob. That's because they've never seen a topflight tournament. Lobbing is standard practice among the stars, always has been, and always will be. The player who tries to burn everything past opponents at the net isn't a he-man. He's just a dope.

Even a tall, powerful athlete, with a thundering overhead game and lots of speed at covering court, is in bad trouble when he encounters an artful lobber. How did little Bobby Riggs cut big Don Budge to pieces in their professional series? By lobbing to him. When Budge came to the net, Riggs lobbed almost every ball. Budge's net game was useless.

Now, your opponents aren't as dangerous as Budge. Therefore, your lobs don't have to be as good as Riggs's to win. Just send up a skyscraper whenever those sharp volleyers try to set up shop in the forecourt. Don't give them chances to volley. Keep them chasing lobs. What if they do smash them? The average club player misses more smashes than he makes. Every tennis match is lost on errors, not won on aces. See if your triumphant net-stormers don't look less overpowering when they're in the backcourt trying to put away those high balls against two determined retrievers. Remember, it's no cinch to beat two men with an overhead shot from anywhere back of the service line. Your foes may wear themselves to a frazzle trying to do it. Anyhow, they'll be feeling frustrated because you're making them play differently from the way they like to play. Every time they smash one and it goes out, or you send it back, they'll feel more frustrated.

Maybe one of your opponents is poaching at the net when you return service. He's leaping across to cut off your returns. This can be a demoralizing trick. It can lead you into making your returns wider and wider, until they either go out or are easy marks for the poacher's partner as he runs in after serving.

The way to cure a man of poaching is to fire a few down the alley. Remember, the only reason he's giving you so much trouble at the net is that he knows where your return of service is going. He's able to start edging across to intercept it before you even hit the ball. If you put one on the other side of him, he's moving in the wrong direction and probably won't be able to return it at all. Thus your shot, which ordinarily would be risky, becomes a pretty safe one. You have more space than usual to place it down the line because the pest opposite you has been leaving some of that space unguarded. And your ball doesn't have to be specially hard to handle because he's not in position nor in balance to handle it. Fool him once or twice this way, and he won't poach any more because he'll be afraid to leave his alley unguarded.

If You're Missing

Maybe this match is going against you because of your own errors. It isn't the aces of your own opponents, but just your own attempted aces that land outside of court. You're missing set-ups.

There's an answer for that, too. Several answers.

One answer is purely muscular. Loosen up. Quit pressing. Quit trying to blast the other team off the court. Slow down, take some deep breaths, and smooth out your strokes. We went all through this in Chapter 8. Review it mentally now.

The other answer is a tactical one. Change the type of shot you've been trying and missing.

The chances are, your overhead is the department that's gone haywire. You're smashing into the bottom of the net, or into the next court. That happens a lot in middle-class doubles.

Don't let it happen to you any longer. The best way to avoid it is to stop smashing. You don't have to smash to win. George Lott was a deadly doubles player, but he never killed the ball. Ditto for Bobby Riggs. And the same for Bob Lutz, whom I consider one of the great doubles players in modern tennis. To watch Lutz play, you'd think he was just ordinary. No spectacular smashes. No magnificent leaps and dashes. He's great because he's always in position, and always gets the ball back smoothly to the right place. Instead of murdering the ball, he gradually maneuvers his opponents into a spot where they hand him the point. They either hit the ball out, or they send back a weak return that he blocks off gently and neatly, without exerting himself, for a sure ace.

What works for Lutz in his league will work for you in your league. Whenever you get an overhead shot, play it safe. Instead of smashing it with all your might, just push it back, deep down the center. Wait for a glaring opening. It will come. After the ball has gone back and forth a few times, you'll get an overhead shot so easy that you can win without smashing. Simply angle it off to the side.

I don't say that you should never, never, never smash. But I do say that if you're smashing and making errors, you'd better try something else. A common mistake of middle-class doubles players is to smash at the wrong time. They smash much more often than the experts do. They go to the net behind their serve, make the first volley, then smash the lob return—and miss it. Why don't they stop beating themselves? Why don't they wait for a lob that comes down close to the net, where even an inexpert smasher can massacre it?

If your overhead is wild, use it sparingly. Use it only on the easy shots. When you get a lob that isn't too easy, make a safe return. By the time your opponents have lobbed three or four times in one rally, that lovely law of averages will get them in trouble, and they'll be almost sure to lob one out, or lob it so shallow that even Methuselah could put it away.

You also have another choice if your smashes are going badly. Maybe a cunning opponent has decided to take advantage of your erratic overhead and is feeding you a steady diet of lobs (which is exactly what I advised you to do under certain circumstances, as you probably remember reading earlier in this chapter). All right. Now the opposition is giving you some of your own medicine, and it's bitter. Well, let's mix them up. Let's bring them to the net, and see if their overhead is any more accurate than yours! Retreat to the baseline for a while and start lobbing to them. Pull them up into the forecourt. Lob them to death. Tempt them to smash. There's an excellent chance that their overhead will be even worse than yours—particularly if they're a pair of patient lobbers who like to play a waiting game, and customarily hang around the baseline sending up lobs until the opposition misses a smash. Remember, the trick of turning defeat into victory is to make your opponents play in a style to which they're not accustomed. That's why the best way to confound a couple of lobbers is to force them to play in the forecourt. This would be suicide in good doubles, but it's sometimes salvation in the middle-class game.

Find Their Soft Spots

Maybe your opponents are beating you, and you don't know how. You and your partner are playing as well as usual. There's nothing spectacularly successful about the other team's game. It's a fairly even fight, but they seem to have an edge. Why? There's no obvious reason.

In a match this close, two or three points can mean the set. A moment comes when you're behind 30–40 on your own service. The loss of one point here means a service break. But if the point goes your way, the game is deuced, and you're better than an even bet to win it. If you've ever studied the point tabulations of a 6–4 or 6–3 set which was decided by one service break, you've probably discovered that the winners got only a few more points than the losers.

Now, with only a few extra points making the difference between a win and a loss, brains will always tip the balance. Start thinking!

You probably have great difficulty in doing any constructive thinking on the tennis court. If you're like most middle-class players, you never think when you're playing—except to worry about your own backhand, and whether your serve is working today, and why in blazes don't your volleys behave better?

You never think about what the other team is doing. You never plan where to place the ball. You just shoot it back somewhere, anywhere, and a half minute later you have no idea where that ball went, nor how it was returned, nor why. You never look for your opponents' weaknesses. In other words, you're playing tennis with about one-fiftieth of your brain power.

If you used a few more fractions of your memory and intellect, you'd lick most of the players who now beat you regularly. You could win all the close sets that you now lose. Those extra two or three points would go your way, if you only spotted one little weakness—just one—and took advantage of it.

It isn't easy to think, if you're not in the babit. You'll have to take yourself in hand. Make yourself quit fretting about your own errors, and concentrate instead on the other fellow's errors. Why does he make them? What shots give him trouble? What are his favorite shots, and how can you avoid giving him a chance to use them?

If you've previously read Chapter 3 and taken it to heart, this will come naturally to you by now. Even so, anticipation is harder in doubles than singles because there's a wider variety of situations, they come and go more quickly, and there are two opponents to scout instead of one.

Instead of looking for dozens of weak spots, and remembering them, as the experts do, just look for one or two. They'll be enough to give you the few extra points you need in a close set. Later on, as you get used to observing and remembering, you'll be able to spot more and more chinks in your opponents' armor.

I'm going to give you a list of things to look for in scouting an opposing doubles team. I know you won't be able to remember this list in the heat of battle. But if you select one or two items before you even step onto the court and look exclusively for those, you'll probably do all right. Close your eyes and stick a pin in the page, if you like, and start scouting for whatever weakness is named where the pin lands.

Does one of your opponents have a weak serve? Then move in closer to receive it.

Does he always serve to your forehand side, or always to your backhand, in one of the service courts? Then be ready for it. You can even edge over a bit more to that side, if you don't make it too obvious.

Is one opponent weak in returning service? Then move up nearer the net when your partner is serving to him.

Does an opponent have a faulty backhand? Then pound it.

Does he have a steady backhand, but hits it with a slice? Then pound it anyhow and rush in to volley his returns because a slice produces a rising ball which is easy to volley.

Where does each man smash? The average player always smashes to the same side. Cover that side and you'll drive him mad.

Which of your two opponents has the weaker overhead? Even if there's only a small difference, capitalize on it. Send every lob to that man. Just one or two more errors may cost them a crucial game.

Does one player stay a little too far back when he's at the net? Then hit low to his feet and move in.

Or does he crowd the net too closely? Then put a fast lob just over his head. Ted Schroeder and Jack Kramer used to specialize in lobbing their service returns low over the server's partner, and every time they did it they won the point outright.

Does one player hit a feeble overhead? Then lob to him, and move in to cut off his return at the net.

Maybe one player never lobs. Or usually flubs it when he tries. Then grab the net every time you send the ball to him.

Does one player have a serve that's really hard to handle? Try backing up and lobbing skyscrapers. It's better than making errors.

Is one player anxious about his alley? Always sidling over to protect it? Then there's an opening in the center. Put the ball there. But not too often, or he'll close the gap. Just use it occasionally, when you really need a point.

Are they good retrievers, who keep getting the ball back no matter how hard you smash? Then don't smash so hard. Save your strength and your temper. Just toy with them a while, and wait for a ball you're sure you can't miss.

How are their backhands against a high ball? Test them. You may uncover a glaring weakness you never suspected.

Are they having trouble with your serve? If not, start mixing them up. Put more slice on your serve, or less. Deliberately vary the direction of your serves—to their backhand once or twice, then to their forehand. Give them a slow serve, so you can keep it really low. Many players can't return a low serve.

Is one player faster afoot than the other? Then make his partner do the running.

The stars think about all these questions in every match. They remember every weakness shown by their opponents. Yet few tennis stars are mental giants. If they can be brainy, so can you. It's all a matter of habit. Get in the habit of thinking!

14 / Partner Trouble?

Where to Put Him

It's a helpless feeling, isn't it, when you're saddled with a partner who constantly muffs shots that ought to be easy? The ghastly realization that your teammate is a lemon and that the other team is going to pour the heat on him gives you an attack of sinking spells—because there doesn't seem to be anything you can do about it. You can't play his shots for him. You can't order him off the court. You can't even look daggers at him, if you're using your head, because you know this would only make him play more erratically than ever. So you feel as if you're bound and gagged.

However, be of good cheer. You're not as helpless as you think. You can do some masterminding which will minimize your partner's weaknesses, no matter what they are. Whether he can't run, can't serve, can't return serve, can't volley, or can't smash, there's a strategy to save the situation. There are tricks by which you can guide the play toward his strong points and away from his vulnerable spots: not on every play, of course, but much more frequently than you'd imagine. Few doubles players know how to protect a partner's weaknesses. Once you understand this gentle art, you'll probably be a popular partner and a formidable opponent.

The first principle to understand is this: the weaker player should be on the right, the stronger one on the left. In other words, if you have a flat tire for a partner, give him the forehand half of the court to cover, while you take the backhand side.

There are several reasons for this. A weak player usually has an absolutely putrid backhand drive, which you'll need to cover up as much as possible. You don't want him to be forced to return any serves with his backhand. Now, if he receives service in his forehand court, the server hasn't much chance of placing the ball on his backhand. It's almost impossible for anyone except a real sharpshooter.

In serving to the backhand court, obviously it's a different story. Then the server can move over toward his own backhand alley and fire a diagonal serve which often will hit in the receiver's backhand corner and pull him wide across his backhand alley. That receiver had better be you, if you have a passable backhand and your partner hasn't.

You needn't worry too much about your partner's backhand when he's at the net. An ordinary volley isn't too hard to make with a backhand. Just stick your racket up there, and you've done it. Almost any mediocre player can volley just as well on either side of him. As for rallies when you're both in backcourt, if a ball comes down the center between the two of you, he should keep his feeble backhand stroke out of the picture and let you return the ball with your forehand.

There's still another reason why the stronger player takes the left-hand side of the court: he'll have more smashes to make on that side. When a team is at the net and a high ball in the center gives them a chance to smash, not even a lunatic is going to try a backhand smash when his partner can reach the ball for a forehand smash. Therefore the man on the left takes not only the high balls in his half of the court, but also the ones anywhere in the center sector. The other man smashes only when the ball is so far on the forehand side that his partner definitely can't reach it.

This holds true in the Wimbledon center court just as firmly as it does on the dirt court at Camp Winnepodunk. Even when both men are international champions, whichever one is the more powerful always plays the backhand side. George Lott, master of finesse that he was, took the forehand and put Stoefen or Van Ryn or Hennessy on the backhand so they could put the ball away with their sledgehammer smashes. Don Budge invariably played on the left, Mako on the right when they were winning their world doubles titles. Vines and Shields were the power players who did the smashing while their respective partners, Gledhill and Parker, made the soft subtle placements that worked the enemy out of position. Next time you see a high-quality doubles match, if you want to know which member of the team is the smasher and which is the fencer, just see where they're playing. The one on the left is the power, the one on the right is the finesse.

Of course, I'm talking only about position when receiving serves. Naturally, when their team is serving, the two partners have to switch sides on each serve. If the server starts the point from the forehand side, he certainly isn't going to try to switch over and cover the backhand side after serving. Each man will stay on the side he starts from, except in the infrequent cases when one of them crosses over to take a lob, as described in Chapter 11.

If your partner has an unpredictable overhead or a nonexistent smash, you'll just have to grin and bear it during the games when your team is serving. On alternate points he'll inevitably be playing the backhand half of the court. However, this still won't give him many ground strokes to hit with his backhand since most of those come into play in returning service. His overhead is another matter. If he can't put the ball away, or if he's hitting too many out of court, your move is to suggest that he change his tactics. Get him to push the ball back, safely and softly, instead of trying to kill it. Persuade him that he'll be smarter to keep the ball in play than to try to win the point with a shot that goes outside. Sell him on placing the ball instead of smashing it. That's what the wizards such as Dent and Alexander and Van Dillen and Smith do, when they get a difficult high ball. They know they can't kill it, so they don't try.

If He Can't Play the Net

Some players won't go to the net. They just don't enjoy seeing a ball come smoking in at them like a tracer bullet. They're too flustered and frightened to cope with it. Sometimes they even have a complex about it, from getting hurt by a hard-hit ball long ago, and really are psychologically incapable of staying at the net. There are a few in every tennis club.

Maybe you've drawn one for a partner. Or maybe you've drawn someone who isn't afraid, but just has slow reflexes that he can't volley or dash into the forecourt. Whatever the reason, you'll need to pull some special strategy out of your bag of tricks.

Of course, part of the time you can use the one-up-and-one-back formation, with you at the net (see Chapter 11). But when you're serving, this won't work since you have to start the point from the baseline. What to do?

Just make sure you send over as good a serve as you can—then hang back, play defensively, and watch for chances to make a lightning dash into the forecourt all by yourself. It can be done. Naturally you'll have to run farther and faster than usual, but if you're crafty you can still outmaneuver your opponents. Your strategy is to keep shuttling forward and back in your half of the court—racing to the net whenever your partner makes a good shot, retreating to the baseline whenever he makes a weak one.

Be especially vigilant for your opponents' mistakes. If they send a feeble shot to your partner, start moving in before he even hits it, because the odds are that he'll hit a good one, and if he does you'll want to be in the forecourt to powder their next return. If one of your opponents has a particularly weak backhand, you should get on top of the net whenever he has to use that backhand. And naturally you'll try to force him to use it as often as possible.

Advance or retreat with every shot. If the shot is a fairly hard one to your partner, back up a bit. You know what's likely to happen: he'll make a return that gives the other team a chance to rush the net. Any time they're at the net, you'd better be well back behind the baseline, ready to chase their volleys and smashes.

Any weak shot to you or your partner should be your signal to advance—just a little if it's only slightly weak, all the way if it's very weak. Likewise, anything feeble from your side of the net means you should retreat instantly. How far you retreat depends on how feeble the shot is.

Whenever you are at the net, remember to move toward the side where the ball is so you're in the center of the area through which it can possibly be returned.

Just on general principles, move somewhere, every time the ball is hit. Remember what I told you in the last chapter, about how bothersome it is to play against somebody whose whereabouts are always changing? Now is the time to wring the last point from that principle. Use it every second. Be elusive. Keep feinting. Pretend to start forward, then back up, or vice versa. Be unpredictable. Be peripatetic. You'll find that your opponents can be startled into making a lot of silly mistakes!

If He Can't Serve

You'll also find that this same strategy of rattling your opponents can compensate for some sadly insipid serves by your partner. If he can't serve, you should become a poacher. (Poaching is good in any match, but it's essential with a weak-serving partner.)

Try to get him to place his serve as accurately as he can, even if there's no zing to it at all. If you can be sure that it's going to one side or the other, this will help your poaching because you can crowd over farther to the side before he hits his serve. When the return comes back, try your fiercest to cut it off at the net.

Even if you knock it a mile outside, or into the bottom of the net, get your racket on it anyhow. Even if the return is clear out of reach, throw yourself at it. Try for everything.

Your objective is to worry the receiver. If he sees that you're getting his returns, or almost getting them, he'll start pushing his returns farther and farther to the side to keep them out of your reach. Every now and then he'll hit one out of court altogether. The ones that do go in will be so far to the side that your partner will have a beautiful chance to ram them straight down the alley.

This sometimes works well even when your server is so erratic that nobody has any idea where he'll put the ball. Your furious lunges to one side or the other will cause you to make a lot of errors, but you'll compensate for them by throwing the receivers off their game.

However, one thing to remember is that a receiver can do almost anything with a weak serve, if he puts his mind to it. He can send it to either side of you, he can drive it deep or shallow, he can put a short lob just over your head or a high one to the baseline. So don't be caught napping. Study your opponents. Take note of whether they like to lob. If they do, you'll have to try your poaching from a point a little farther back from the net than usual. When your partner is a weak server and the receiver is a good lobber, don't move in any closer than a foot inside the service line to start play.

Take a note of the way they drive when they're returning service. Are they capable of making that difficult down-the-line return? If so, be ready for it. If not, camp nearer the center line, and get ready to throw yourself far into the other service court to volley their cross-court return.

Take note of their backhands. Can you spot a weakness there? Then coach your partner to try to place his serve on that backhand as often as possible, while you move farther over to that side and closer to the net so you can climb aboard a high soft return. Poaching works best against a mushy backhand.

Don't poach on every shot, though. Mix them up. Pretend to poach, without actually doing it, sometimes. Start moving at unexpected times: on one serve dart across as soon as the ball leaves your partner's racket, on the next one stand motionless until the receiver starts to hit it. Never stand in the same spot twice when your partner is serving. Edge this way or that. Keep leaning in various directions, or shifting your weight without moving your feet, sometimes crouching, sometimes standing straight, feinting and bobbing and lunging. A clever poacher can sometimes drive a very good player completely crazy. Try it.

If He's Tired

If your partner had too much fun at the soda fountain the night before, or if he's not as young as he used to be, then Mother Nature is going to take her toll in the later stages of a hectic match. A partner who was a ball of fire in the first set may be burnt out by the fourth.

When this happens, here's what you can do. Have him stand farther back when he receives service so he can take a slower and easier stroke. Whenever he returns the serve well, you should charge the net alone and gamble on putting the ball away. Make the opposition concentrate its fire on you, and try to shorten the rallies.

When you receive service, station him close to the net, and fairly far to the side. The more exhausted he is, the closer to the net he should stand, and the closer to the sideline. The result will be that the opposition can't afford to shoot anything at him. Obviously, if he's on top of the net, all he has to do is stick up his racket. If he only gets the wood on the ball, it's still going to bounce back over, and probably drop dead before they can reach it. The closer to the sideline he is, the less chance the enemy has to blaze a passing shot to either side of him. Just keep him up there at the front corner, and cover the rest of the court yourself. Of course this means that you'll practically be playing singles, since you've placed your partner in a spot where no balls will come to him. But that's better than leaving him out there in exposed territory where they can take advantage of his enfeebled condition. It's your best way out of a tough predicament.

When he's serving, tell him to stay back at the baseline, while you poach on every return of service. If they get on past you, back up fast and pray that your partner can lob it too deep for them to smash.

Keep Him Out of Harm's Way

As a general rule, if there's anything glaringly wrong with your partner, you should give him as little territory to cover as possible, and extend your own theater of operations. Roam all over the court. Make them hit to you instead of to him.

Thus, if he's missing all his volleys, tell him to stand closer to the net, while you lurk farther back. They don't dare let him volley if he's right on top of the net, because he can't miss them. Instead, they'll either lob over him, or angle a diagonal shot across the part of the net he can't reach. In either case, you have a good chance to retrieve it.

If he's messing up his return of service, tell him to back away farther from the net, and lob whenever he can. Meanwhile you'll also stand farther back than usual, but both of you should be ready to rush in whenever he makes a good return.

If they've discovered that he has no overhead, and are lobbing him to death, tell him not to smash, but to push the ball back safely and conservatively. Move him over farther toward the sideline, while you occupy the center, so that you can take more of the lobs. Whenever a lob comes over that you think you've a chance to get, yell for it and take it. Every doubtful one should be yours.

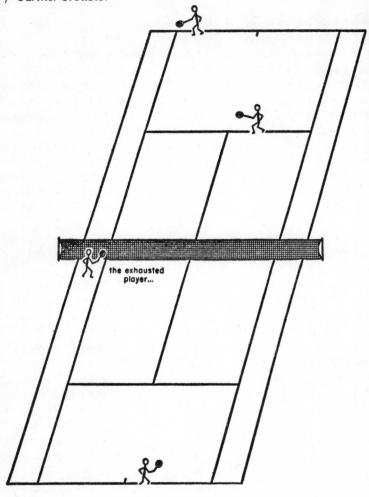

Figure 19. When your partner is exhausted or
weak, place him close to net and close to sideline.
This way he will receive very few shots. You, of
course, must cover the whole court.

Don't Let Him Chop

Every now and then you'll see a player who has just one serious flaw: he chops his forehand. Such players are fairly common. They have a decent backhand and serve, they do all right on volleys and smashes, and as singles players they're rather tough to beat. But when they get into a game of doubles, a smart opponent will cut them to pieces just by capitalizing on that forehand chop.

A chop always produces a rising ball. So what happens? The server gives him a ball on his forehand, charges the net, and chortles with glee as the chopped return arches upward toward him. He smashes it, or at least volleys it sharply downward, and the point is probably over.

Don't let this happen when the chopper is on your team. If he is approximately as good a player as you, put him on the backhand side to receive service. Then he can take every serve on his backhand, and they won't be able to get at his forehand. When a ball comes deep down the middle during a rally, don't let him have it. Take it yourself on your backhand.

Furthermore, you'd better coach him to lob, or else make his chop so gentle that it drops at the opponents' feet, on the rare occasions when he does have to hit off his right side. Explain to him that a forehand chop is a handy stroke in singles, but suicide in doubles. If you're at all diplomatic, you can make him see the light.

If He's Left-Handed

The southpaw doubles player is a special problem. For some reason that I've never quite figured out, practically all the left-handed players I've known have had weak backhands. They just can't develop that stroke, somehow, even if they're tournament players who work on their game daily.

Furthermore, they usually seem to be rather futile at forehand volleying. Don't ask me why. With these two exceptions, they have as good strokes as anyone else in their own league—and they have a more dangerous serve than a right-hander, in doubles. Why? Because when they serve from the left-hand court, to an opponent's backhand court, the left-handed serve gives them a wider angle. They can angle the serve across court more sharply into the backhand corner and pull the receiver farther out of court than a right-handed server can hope to.

If your partner is a southpaw, put him on the backhand side to receive service. He'll have to return too many serves with his backhand if he receives in the other court. During the rallies, any balls down the middle should be yours—again, because you don't want him to use his backhand.

When he serves, he should serve from the same spots that a right-hander would. But, as his partner, your position should be slightly different. On the odd points, when his serve is almost certain to break wide to the receiver's backhand, you'll want to be farther over to that side to intercept his return.

It all comes down to this: whatever a player's weaknesses are, his partner can spot them and cover them up if he just uses his intellect. Get intellectual!

15 / Mixed Doubles

Formula for Fun

Mixed doubles has lately become the most popular of all forms of tennis. It's a great social game, a pleasant way to get acquainted with players at your tennis club or at a resort or even in impromptu pairings at public courts. Some tennis clubs now have a twilight mixed doubles tourney every fortnight, and at some of these clubs it outdraws all other events staged there.

Many married couples have made a change in their way of spending a social evening. Instead of playing bridge with friends, or going to the theater, or giving a dinner party, they'll often ring up another couple and spend the evening playing mixed doubles.

Mixed doubles has zoomed into popularity even for spectators. In the World Team Tennis league, one-fifth of each team match is mixed doubles; the final set of the evening, which often decides the match, is always mixed doubles. Why? Because promoters find that galleries like this best. Mixed doubles has more variety (and probably more human interest) than the other events.

Charity tournaments at which celebrities are the gate attractions usually consist mostly of mixed doubles—again, because this kind of competition sells more tickets. And even in the big tournaments that determine national rankings, the stars strive vigorously to win the mixed doubles title. To me this is the most striking change of all. Until a few years ago the big-time players all ducked the mixed doubles if they could; tournament organizers had to pressure them to get a respectable entry list for this event, because they considered it a dull and meaningless nonhappening. How times have changed!

The main reason for the change, I suppose, is the vastly increased number of good women players. The great national upsurge in feminine sport, the increased emphasis on athletics for girls from grammar school up, has equalized what sometimes was a rather lopsided style of tennis. We often used to see two dominant males bounding all over the court while their feminine partners seemed content to be more ornamental than combative. But now it isn't unusual to see a wife playing better tennis than her husband.

Aside to the Women

This next section is addressed specifically to feminine players. (The whole book is aimed just as much at you as at the men, because its advice applies equally to both sexes. But in this section, as in Chapter 20, I'll emphasize pointers that I've found are particularly helpful to women players.)

Let's assume you're looking ahead to a mixed doubles session. If it's important enough to spend time in practicing for, here's what your preparation should emphasize:

Work on your lob, and plan to use it often. Smart doubles teams do a lot of lobbing; dumb teams do very little. Remind yourself to move toward the net whenever you drive opponents back with a good lob.

Work on your overhead, if you expect to be playing against a smart team—because you'll get plenty of lobs in that case, and if they find you're erratic in returning them they'll lob you to death.

Practice your first serve. In doubles, getting the first serve in is vital. But it shouldn't be a bullet serve that gives you no time to move forward before the return is at your feet. It should be a slicing or arching serve that kicks wide to the receiver's backhand.

Work on wide cross-court shots. The doubles court is wider, of course, so you'll have more opportunity to pull your opponents out of the court with low, shallow drives and volleys into the alleys. Plan to return all serves cross-court (for reasons explained in Chapters 10 and 11). Cross-court is the name of the game in doubles.

Fix certain plans in your mind, so you'll avoid certain common errors by doubles players of both sexes. Resolve that when your partner is receiving service, you'll move up just inside the service line, and will always look back to watch your partner getting ready to hit it. If you see he'll have trouble with it, hustle back on the defense, so you'll be in position to retrieve that volley that is sure to come when a doubles receiver makes a weak return. Conversely, if you see your partner is making a good return, remember to move farther forward to do some volleying yourself.

In serving, resolve to start forward instantly instead of just craning your neck to see whether the serve goes in. Even if you're not a sharp volleyer, you should be at least a few feet inside the baseline when your serve reaches the receiver.

Resolve to study both your opponents as they serve, and see where their serves usually land, so you can position yourself more strategically.

Make a mental note that whenever your partner serves, you should be in the center of the service court, about halfway between the net and the service line—and that after his serve crosses the net, you should edge over toward the inside, where most of the action is. Don't fall into the habit of hanging around the alley just because that big space on the outside looks so unprotected. Few players try the difficult shot down the alley, and you can easily block it if they do, even from the center of the service court.

And now a word about psychology.

Friction between mixed doubles partners has blighted a few romances and more than a few marriages. In the heat of play, it's all too easy for partners to snap, snarl, and glare at each other. The better we know someone, of course, the less likely we are to mind our manners under stress. That's why some married couples never team with each other on the tennis court (nor at the bridge table).

By using your tact and perceptiveness, you can bring out the best in your partner, whether he's your husband or fiancé or just an acquaintance. Resist all temptations to give him an icy glance or a sharp admonition, even if that's what you're getting from him. You can settle him down and actually get him playing better if you keep smiling, sympathizing, praising every good shot he makes. Don't gripe. Chuckle! Remember that this is supposed to be a friendly game, and you're both on the court to have fun.

The hardest part will be keeping your cool if he's irascible, or if he tries to cover too much of the court. But a soft answer turneth away wrath—

and a little tact can induce a partner to change tactics. Just ask, "Do you think we might do better if we change and try it this way?" It's more diplomatic, obviously, to say "we" instead of "you" in making any remark which might seem like criticism.

If you're a better player than your male partner, should you take the left-hand side of the court? (Remember that standard doubles strategy is to put the stronger player on the left, and that all experienced players are aware of this.) It depends on whether you want to soothe the male ego. He may be humiliated if friends see him on the right-hand side of the court, in the traditional spot of the weaker player, when his partner is a woman. Some tactful women always take the forehand side when they have a male partner, even if he's eighty years old. Others don't. Consider your partner's temperament and your own, and do whatever you think best.

Aside to the Men

Too often the male member of a mixed doubles team sets out to show everyone what a great big wonderful athlete he is. He hits bullet serves and overhead smashes—which annoy his opponents—and he tries to cover the whole court—which infuriates his partner.

By the end of the set all three people may have decided never to speak to him again, and his two opponents may also be mad at each other because they let him beat them. Someone ought to tell him to stay out of mixed doubles—because mixed doubles (anywhere below the big-time tournament level) are strictly for fun.

If you insist on playing to win, nobody will have any fun. Playing to win means pounding the opposing woman, smashing for aces whenever you can, probing for weak spots, pouncing on balls in your partner's territory. That's the way to win, except in the rare cases where the woman has made herself an outstanding athlete. So, if you keep hammering the ball at the woman on the other side of the net, concentrating on her weakest spots, you'll win plenty of points. And if you make your own partner stand off to the side, right on top of the net where nobody dares hit a ball at her, you'll be able to monopolize the play and prevent the opposition from bombarding her.

Yes, that's the way to win. And it's the way a professional match is played, or a grudge match. But few women enjoy it. They're either bombarded relentlessly, or they're shoved into a corner and ignored. Not many men really enjoy this sort of game either.

In social mixed doubles, the well-mannered males send the women the kind of balls that are likely to be handled capably. If you want the women to enjoy themselves, forget about your big serve. When you get a chance to put the ball away, don't. Instead, aim it back where you know the opposition can get it. You ought to enable the women to get lots of action.

After all, tennis is a game of skill. Use your skill in aiming your shot where your opponents can reach it if they try hard. If your female opponent has a good forehand, hit the balls there, and you won't need to worry about slowing them down too much, because many women have good forehands. If she hasn't developed a powerful overhead smash, you should resist the temptation to lob to her. Lob to her partner, but give her the balls she can volley or drive. If she's weak at the net, keep the ball deep in her back court. If she likes to play net, give her some rising balls occasionally so she'll have the satisfaction of climbing on top of them.

When you're serving to a woman, work on your control. Practice placing the ball where she likes it. When you're serving to a man, hit your best licks. During a rally, if there's any doubt about whether you or your partner should take a shot, call to her to take it.

Make up your mind that you'll use the session to practice your own weakest strokes. Do everything the hard way. If your forehand is your best side, take as many shots as possible on your backhand. If you're not much of a volleyer, rush the net whenever there's half a chance. If you're a good volleyer, make it tough on yourself by standing farther than usual from the net, or closer to it. Or get too far to the side, so you leave an inviting opening; then you'll really have to leap when they shoot at it.

You can prolong a rally indefinitely, even though you're hitting the ball sharply, if you keep placing it on the woman's strong side at about waist height. You can run like mad after easy lobs if you've deliberately crowded the net too closely. And you can give yourself a good workout chasing the feeblest drop shots if you hang back behind the baseline.

If your side begins to fall behind in the score, turn on a little pressure.

Dink the ball at the opposing woman's backhand. Drop it at her feet. Put a quick lob just over her head. Do some poaching when she receives service. Start using your best shots instead of your poorest ones. Pour the heat on your male opponent's weakness, whatever it is. When the score is even again, go back to being gallant. But don't make either transition abrupt.

Mixed Doubles for Blood

If you're playing a tournament match, or a social one where considerations of love or hate make it imperative for you to win by as overwhelming a score as possible, you still should be pleasant, although efficient instead of easygoing.

Above all, encourage your partner. Enthuse over her good shots, sympathize with her bad ones. Talk to her constantly. Never get mad or pessimistic.

As for your strategy, it's all designed to exploit the opposition's weakness and protect your partner. Keep firing the ball at the other woman whenever you can. Concentrate on her overhead and her backhand. Make her run incessantly. Find the man's shortcomings, too, and work on them.

Don't let the other team make a patsy out of your partner. Put her so close to the net that she can't miss, and so far to the side that she'll never get in your way. Then simply proceed to play singles, covering the whole court yourself.

Your male opponent, if he's at all smart, will put his female partner in the same spot. Your answer is to force him to run himself to death. Put the ball in one alley and then in another. Pull him into the forecourt with dink shots, then chase him back with lobs. Of course, when his female partner is serving, he can't keep her out of harm's way, and this is your chance to drive the ball back at her feet or her backhand every time she gets it over the net.

If you play with a woman who has strong ground strokes, try the old-fashioned one-up-and-one-back style. Let her stay at the baseline on the forehand side (assuming her forehand is stronger than her backhand) while you take the net on the backhand side. If you crowd in close, the opponents will probably try to keep the ball away from you by driving to your partner. This gives her a chance to use her favorite ground stroke constantly, and may win a lot of points for you.

If your female partner can't come to the net with her serve, you should fall back a little after her serve. When your team receives service, you should always take the backhand court and let her receive in the righthand one. Play just as you would in men's doubles with an inferior or exhausted partner (in case you've been skipping chapters, Chapter 14 told just how to handle such painful occasions).

Above all try to keep the level of sportsmanship high whenever you're playing, either for fun or for blood. It doesn't hinder your chances if you're genial instead of grim. It doesn't do any harm to call "nice shot" to your opponents now and then. And you may even steer the dialogue clear of such arguments and recriminations as once led a player to draw himself up and reprimand his male opponent sternly: "Sir, you are speaking to my wife—and to the mother of my children."

16 / Two Heads Are Better–

Collusion, Not Collision

A pair of moderately good tennis players, if they happen to be strong-minded and self-willed individualists, can team up in doubles and look about as efficient as Rowan and Martin. It happens every day.

Doubles partners all over the country unconsciously use the system of "every man for himself"—and wonder why their defense has as many holes as a cribbage board. They can't seem to grasp the simple fact that a doubles match is no place for rugged individualism.

Here's what happens constantly at tennis clubs and public courts. One man decides to rush the net while his partner is deciding to retreat. Or one crosses the court to retrieve a lob, but his buddy doesn't budge from the forecourt on that same side. Or a ball comes down the middle and both men charge for it, colliding heavily. Next time each waits for the other to take it, and it drops untouched. On the next one, both partners start for it, then see that the other has started too; they both stop again, and the ball falls between them once more.

After a series of these starts and stops and collisions, interspersed with one-man dashes which leave half the court uncovered, an electrician could attach a wire to either partner and light up the city of Chicago. Each man blames the other. He blames him not only for poor teamwork, but for poor shots, poor court-covering, poor manners, and moral turpitude. Neither man gets mad at himself for missing shots or getting caught out of position. But what he thinks about his partner, for the same kind of mistakes, couldn't pass through the mails. Time and again I've seen partners so furious at the end of a "friendly" game of doubles that they wouldn't speak to each other for days afterward. "I'll never play with him again!" is a stock phrase around every club. Such resolutions seldom last for more than a week, but still they give a lot of men high blood pressure. I hate to see these things happen because they're not only harmful but easily avoidable.

If two partners would only put their heads together before they go on the court, and work out a few simple agreements, they'd save each other all kinds of pain and strain. Tennis teamwork isn't hard to achieve. It just takes a little mutual forethought.

You never see two expert players stand expectantly waiting for each other to go after a ball. You never catch them both covering the same half of the court at the same time, or playing one-up-and-one-back. You never hear them bawl each other out. Why not? Simple. They understand each other—even if it's the first time they've ever played together.

You don't have to be psychic, or a Phi Beta Kappa, to set up a smooth working arrangement with a partner. Tennis stars aren't usually mental marvels. Between the ears, they're just normal guys. But they all follow a universal system of doubles teamwork, as clear as the red-and-green traffic lights on any boulevard, so they don't get tangled up. You and your partners can be just as systematic, if you'll hold a brief council of war before starting to play.

Whose Ball?

The first thing you'd better agree on is who should take balls that come between you. When you're both at the net, volleying hot and heavy, a lot of returns will whiz right down the middle, within reach of either of you. Who takes them? There's only a fraction of a second to decide.

Here's the rule to follow: When volleying, whichever player hits one ball should hit the next one too, if he can reach it.

For example, you're serving from the forehand side. You put the ball over, move in, take the return with a backhand volley or half volley, then move in farther. The defenders send a sizzling shot through the center. Even though it's on your partner's forehand and your backhand (which we'll assume is not a thing of beauty), it's up to you to make another backhand volley. If there's a long rally and the opposition keeps trying to pass you through the center, you keep on volleying with your backhand.

By the same token, if your partner had started the exchange with a forehand, he would take all those same balls on his forehand. Everything depends on who hit the first shot.

This is how big-time players avoid confusion at the net. It works just as neatly in middle-class doubles. You may wonder why the rule calls for one player to keep hitting continuously, instead of letting partners alternate on those in-between shots, or letting them go to whichever partner can put his forehand on them. The theory behind the rule is this: When you hit one volley successfully, you're hot. You can do it the same way a split-second later. It's a matter of rhythm. Just by repeating a stroke several times in quick succession, you get into a pattern and the stroke is easy for you. The rapid-fire volleying at the net keeps you keyed up and on your toes, so you're ready and eager for another volley. Your partner isn't quite as hot, if he hasn't hit the last shot or two, and therefore he wouldn't have quite as good prospects of making a sharp return. The difference is slight, but it pays off.

However, if you and your buddy are in the back court, playing defensively, the rule is different. Now, when either a volley or a smash or a lob comes down the middle, and both of you have about equal chances of getting it, the man on the left should always take it, so he can use his forehand. Occasionally, in the higher strata of tennis, this rule is changed if one partner happens to have a Big Bertha backhand and the other is just ordinary with forehands. Then they'll agree ahead of time that the middle shots should go to the backhander. But in once-a-week tennis, where nearly everyone's forehand is his stronger side, that's the stroke to use.

Yell for It

Of course, most balls aren't going to come right smack dab between you and the other fellow. They'll be slightly to one side or the other. But there won't be time to unroll a measuring tape and see which of you is closer to the ball. Never mind. If you're at the net, and it's your turn to volley, go after any ball that's anywhere within your reach. No matter if it's closer to your partner than you—if you can get it, it's yours. Take it.

But at the same time, yell "Mine."

This business of calling your shots is important. It removes the doubt from your partner's mind. It's collision insurance. Always yell for the ball, at the earliest possible instant, when it's between the two of you and you're going to volley it.

Never say "Take it" or "Yours" for a fast ball coming between you at the net. Your partner won't be able to react fast enough. The ironclad rule, in volleying, is that whichever player is taking the shot should give oral notice of his intention. Thus, if both players start for the ball, and both yell for it, whichever one yells first has the right of way.

The rule is reversed in chasing lobs. If there's doubt about who should go after a lob, a player who would have to hit it on his backhand, or who doesn't think he can get to it as fast as his partner, should not only give his partner precedence but should tell him so—as early, and as loudly as possible. There may be times when you're at the net, and somebody flips a quick lob just over your head. Maybe you start to try for it, and then see that you can't get quite high enough. Yell "Take it" to your partner instantly.

If you both start after the ball, as soon as one of you sees that he's a bit farther from it, he should call "Yours" and abandon the chase. But if you are convinced that you can take it, and your partner is after it also, there's no reason why you shouldn't say "I've got it" if he hasn't said anything. That should be his signal to stop running—and will be, if you've agreed on these signals beforehand.

The one thing that mustn't happen is an Alphonse and Gaston act where you both start for the ball, see that your partner has started too, and both stop. When you're chasing a ball, never slacken speed until you've called "Yours" or your partner has said "I'll take it." If both of you think the other guy ought to try for it, neither of you can stop running until somebody has said something. Then, whoever concedes the ball to his partner first is the one entitled to relax.

On any high ball that isn't too high or too deep to smash, remember that whichever partner is the powerhouse should do the smashing. That's why the harder hitter is always in the backhand side of the court to receive service—so that he can use his forehand to smash all the in-between high ones. When your team is serving, and the slugger happens to be on the forehand side, he should still do the smashing if he can get his forehand on the ball, or if he happens to be one of those rarities who can smash well with his backhand. If not, the weaker hitter must smash (or stroke the ball back safely, if he knows his overhead is erratic) whenever a high ball is on his forehand.

When to Trade Sides

You occasionally see two sharp doubles players switch sides during a rally. Maybe you haven't noticed when, or why, they do this. Here's their system.

Sometimes a deep lob sails toward one corner. The player in the other half of the court may have a better chance to handle it, for any of several reasons. Maybe he's faster afoot than his partner. Or maybe he got an earlier start toward it. Maybe he's the harder hitter, and he sees he can cross over in time to take it with his forehand smash. Maybe he happens to be farther back from the net than his partner, so that his diagonal path to the ball is actually shorter. Anyhow, let's assume that he crosses into his partner's half of the court to cover that lob. This is a perfectly legitimate maneuver which good players use all the time.

What should his partner do? He should head for the baseline too, but should crisscross, away from the ball, so he'll be in position to cover the half of the backcourt that his partner is vacating. This is what all smart players do. The other ones just stand where they are, as if vegetables were growing up their legs, and wait for the partner to cross back again to his original half of the court after returning the lob.

In rushing the net, or retreating from it, both players should surge forward or back simultaneously. As soon as one man makes a move, his partner is supposed to follow his lead. Whichever one starts forward should be able to count on his partner to do the same. Maybe one man sees an opening and decides to come in for a volley. Even if his teammate hasn't seen the opening, or doesn't agree that this is the time to take the offense, he ought to play along with his partner and come in too. Otherwise both men will shortly be waving good-by to the ball. Likewise, if the team is at the net and one member decides it's time to retire, the instant he starts for the baseline the other member should go with him. Whichever player takes the initiative is entitled to expect his partner to support him. Better get this straight with your cohort before you walk on the court with him.

When to Give Advice

Tournament players constantly help their partners by yelling "Out" or "Let it bounce" when they're pretty sure a ball will drop foul. Club players usually keep their mouths shut. Apparently they're afraid of looking bad by giving voice to a wrong guess. They forget that there are plenty of times when they have a better perspective on a ball than the other fellow, and can see that it's going out when he can't. A player whose gaze is glued to a flying ball can't always be sure of the location of the lines. His partner, who can see those lines, should help him by warning him to leave a bad ball alone.

This can win plenty of points for your team. At the net, if a ball comes toward your partner high and very fast, so you're quite sure it will land beyond the baseline if he leaves it alone, yell "Out." If there's any real doubt in your mind, keep silent. "If in doubt, try for the ball" is a sound rule in all sports. But there are any number of times when a sharp-eyed player with good judgment of distance can be sure that a ball is out, while his partner can't. Call those!

Once again, the rule is different on lobs. If in doubt, let them bounce. There's usually plenty of time to hit them on the rebound. A man pursuing a lob is looking toward the sky. He can't tell whether the lob is doubtful, or definitely in. If it's definitely in, the best policy is usually to hit it on the fly, because it will be closer to the net, and the opposition will have less time to get ready for it. But when it's doubtful, the best policy is always to wait and see. Why throw away a possible point by gambling that your opponent's shot was good? Therefore, it's a big help to a man going back under a lob to know whether the ball is uncertain or sure to go in. The partner should always give this help by calling "Let it bounce" if there's any question. The partner's silence should be a signal to hit the ball on the fly if possible.

Advice on strategy should always be given and received freely between partners. If one man notices a weakness in the opposition, or feels that a different strategy would prevent the opponents from capitalizing on their strength, he ought to talk it over with his partner between games. And his partner ought to be willing to try any new tactics suggested. Open-minded give and take is one of the foundations of doubles teamwork. Maybe you think your partner's suggestion won't work. Try it out anyhow, and do your level best to make it work. Otherwise, how can you expect him to cooperate when *you* suggest something?

You'd think that any two people who decided to team up would have a cooperative spirit toward each other. This is almost invariably the case in good doubles. But it's far from invariable in middle-class doubles. You and your partner will have an important advantage over most opponents if you'll just make up your minds that, come hell or high water, you won't get mad at each other. The old maxim, "Divide and rule," works in tennis too. So does "United we stand." Keep yourself and your partner united. Let the other guys be the ones to snarl and glare at each other. The more they're divided, the easier you'll rule them.

I already hammered at this point in the chapter on mixed doubles, where the provocation to get mad is ever present. There are plenty of provocations in males doubles too, and it won't do any harm to remind you once again that the winning combinations are those that keep calm even when the game is going badly. It does you no good whatever to upbraid your partner, nor to bottle up wrath inside yourself. You've got to remember that all pleasantness pays off. If you want to win, stay sweet!

17 / Enlarge Your Arsenal

Strokes for Doubles

For the past seven chapters I've been talking about doubles. If you're still with me, you certainly realize by now that a doubles player needs a larger arsenal of weapons than a singles player. If he can't volley and lob, he's dead. If he doesn't have a half volley, he's in for trouble. If he has no lob-volley, he isn't quite tops.

You've noticed these strokes mentioned frequently in past chapters. But there's been nothing said, yet, about *how* to execute them. Maybe you already know how. On the other hand, maybe you just think you know. You could be wrong, couldn't you? Let's see.

Get up to the net and rally a while, practicing your volleys. Notice what you do when you hit a shoulder-high ball on your left. Do you hit it with the same face of your racket as you use in hitting a ball on your right? The majority of club players do this, without ever realizing they're doing it.

In other words, they don't really make a backhand volley when the ball is close to them. They never turn the backhand face of their racket to the ball except when it's so far to their left that they have to stretch for it. Instead, they raise their right elbow, turn the palm of their right hand toward the ball, and ward it off with a sort of shield-me-from-the-storm gesture.

Are you sure you don't do this? Whenever I start giving volleying lessons to someone, I always ask him whether he volleys that way, and he usually snorts with derision and says, "Of course not." Then I fire a fast ball above his left ear, and his racket flies up to stop it. His arm curves into a horseshoe shape over his head, and he hits the ball with the same face of the racket that he would for a forehand. It's a reflex with about six out of ten players at every club where I've ever coached. How about you? Check yourself and make sure.

Check, too, to see whether the ball is well ahead of you when you volley it. That's where it should be, but usually isn't. Hitting the ball too late is a common fault among club players.

The reason they hit too late is that they draw their racket back in starting the stroke. That's wrong. There shouldn't be any backswing in making a volley. Notice what your racket does the next time you make a volley, and see whether it draws back before starting forward.

Now check your half volley. Do you bend down to make it, or do you stand up straight? You should bend. But probably you don't. The great mass of middle-class players flub their half volleys because they hit with straight knees, straight back, straight elbow, and bent wrist. They stand erect and try to dig the ball out of the ground by pulling up and away from it as they hit. What do you do?

Now try a few practice lobs. Watch your racket to see whether it follows through after meeting the ball. One reason why so many players can't lob accurately is that they stop their racket short, the instant they hit. Follow-through is just as important in lobbing as it is in serving and driving.

When You Volley, Punch!

Let's take these strokes one at a time and analyze them. We'll consider the volley first because it's the most important of all shots in doubles. To win in doubles you must take the net—and to take the net you must volley. Volleying is a lot of fun, once you know how. Learn it right, and you'll have more fun and more victories.

So many club players say to me, "I'm no good at the net because my reactions are too slow. I just can't put my racket on the ball soon enough." Usually, I can prove to these players that they're mistaken.

It isn't a slow reaction that makes them volley poorly. It's drawing the racket back before they hit. Just a fractional backswing, of only a few inches, is enough to make them late in meeting the ball. They hit it when it's beside them, instead of when it's ahead of them, where it should be.

Unless you have such a big opening that you can put the ball away by simply blocking it off, punch into your volley. Push your racket, don't swing it. Make your volley a stabbing *thrust*, not a jerk or flick. Except for a high volley, you should hit with a locked wrist, as if you were planting a straight right-hand punch in somebody's face.

Remember what I said, way back in Chapter 4, about the deadly sin of wrist-flicking when you drive? It's just as sinful in volleying, and just as prevalent. If you slap at the ball with a buggy-whip wrist, you can't aim it. Keep your wrist firm. Step forward to meet the ball, and put your whole arm and shoulder into that punching motion that thrusts your racket in front of the ball. Then aim your shot by tilting the face of your racket. Simply by the angle of impact, you can make the ball ricochet into any part of the court. Try it.

All these things will come more or less naturally if you just concentrate on the one cardinal principle: hit the ball when it's ahead of you.

Think about this every time you're at the net. Go forward to meet the ball, instead of backing away so you have time to swing your racket at it. Intercept it. All you have to do is block the ball off, with that punching motion, and you can angle your racket head to aim the volley wherever you like.

Next time you're watching some average tennis, or playing it, notice how many players are moving backward, away from the net, as they volley. It's that unnecessary backswing of their racket that makes them retreat. By the time anyone has jerked his racket back, and then started it forward again, the ball is likely to be on top of him, or even passing him. Naturally he has to pull himself back in order to gain a fraction of a second to get his racket on the ball. So he hits the ball late, which means he has no control over where it goes.

Make yourself move *at* the ball, instead of away from it. Spear it. When you do this, you can hardly help eliminating that burdensome backswing.

As for the balls that come at you on your left, remember to volley them with a genuine backhand. Turn your right shoulder to the net, and drop your right elbow, so that the back of your hand instead of its palm is toward the net as you volley. Then you'll be hitting the ball with the opposite face of the racket from the one you use for forehand shots.

Force yourself to do this, even when the ball is only an inch to the left of your nose. Once you can break yourself of that bad habit of slapping at a backhand ball with a forehand motion, as if you were beating a rug, you'll rapidly begin to develop a good backhand volley.

The principle of stepping or even jumping diagonally toward the ball, to intercept it while it's still ahead of you, is just as important in backhand volleys as in forehand. Keep the ball between you and the net—never let it be even with you when you hit it. This isn't a matter of fast reaction, particularly. It's a matter of not trying to swing at the ball, but just jabbing your racket in its path, which takes much less time.

One more point about volleying. In doubles, whenever you're up against intelligent players, you'll have to make a lot of low volleys. Smart opponents won't be silly enough to give you many balls at chest height. They'll try to make the ball trickle over, low and slow and shallow, so you're forced to take it knee high, or even off your shoetops. Whenever this happens, and you're trying to volley a low ball, remember one thing: you must bend down for it!

The average player makes a low volley by simply dropping his racket and trying to scoop the ball up, meanwhile standing perfectly erect. No good. You can't see the ball well enough. You're bound to flub it, or give the other team a rising ball. Instead, loosen up your knees and hips. Bend them. Get down low to make that low volley. Punch into it, with a stiff wrist, just as you do for higher volleys. This way you'll be able to produce a shot that hops over the net and drops quickly, not giving the enemy much chance to kill it.

For Half Volleys, Use Your Hips

The same principle applies in half volleys as in low volleys. You must bend over!

Maybe I'd better explain just what a half volley is. The name is confusing. This shot isn't really a volley at all. When you volley, you hit the ball on the fly. But when you half volley, you hit it after it bounces.

A half volley is the stroke you use in trapping a ball just after it lands. You hit it as it starts to rise, while it's still within a few inches of the ground. This is an important stroke in doubles. Many times as you rush the net, the ball will come back at your feet. Sometimes you can reach it quickly enough to volley it. But other times you can't. Either you take it as it bounces, with a half volley, or else it passes you. By the time it's high again, it's beyond you. That's why you need to know how to make a half volley.

There's always a temptation, when a ball reaches you at about ankle height, to let your arm do all the work of scooping it up. An underhand swing, with the body staying erect—and even pulling up and away from the ball—is the natural reaction to a low ball. You want to swing at it as if your racket were a polo mallet.

But this is one of the cases where the natural way isn't the best way. If you stand straight when you hit a half volley, you'll almost certainly hit the ball into the net, or else shovel it up so high that the opposing net man will climb all over it.

The key to a good half volley is in the hips and knees. Bend them. Get your upper body low enough so that you can hit the ball with a normal sidearm stroke, instead of scooping it underarm. Use a short drawback, then "feel" the ball through. Try for a smooth, flowing stroke, with lots of shoulder and lots of follow-through. No jerking or flicking, remember?

You'll probably have trouble with timing when you start to learn this shot. If you're like most players, you're accustomed to hitting every ball as it's dropping. The first few times you try to take a ball on the rise, you may miss it completely. Don't get discouraged. Keep trying, and remember to glue your eyes on the ball. After a while you'll get the knack of trapping the ball just as it comes up off the ground. Once you've caught the timing, all you need for a good half volley is to bend down and stroke it through.

However, even the best players miss this shot more frequently than any other. They just get careless and succumb to the impulse to stay upright and take a polo-player's swat at it, instead of bending over. I've done it myself. I've known Kramer and Riggs to do it. Then they miss the shot and curse themselves afterward. They know why they missed.

Lob-Volley: Handle with Care

The lob-volley is a dangerous weapon. Dangerous to the foe if you use it well, deadly to yourself if you don't.

Obviously, if your lob-volley doesn't go high enough to be out of reach, the man across the net from you will spike it down your throat. However, if you put it safely over his head, and it doesn't go outside, you've aced him. Therefore a lob-volley is strictly a gambler's shot. When you try it, the point is over. Either you ace your opponent, or he kills it.

Furthermore, it's one of the hardest shots to make. You need a really delicate touch. If you don't hit the ball hard enough, your opponent can jump for it and put it away. If you hit it too hard, it sails beyond the baseline. A good way to make your partner boiling mad is to try a lob-volley that doesn't work. To all appearances you've simply handed the other team a point by sending up a pop fly when you should have been volleying at their feet.

Don't try to learn the lob-volley in close matches. Wait until you're in there with much weaker opponents, so you can sacrifice points without making your partner blow a gasket. Then keep trying it until you learn by practice just how hard to stroke the ball.

The technique is similar to volleying. You hit the ball ahead of you, with a locked wrist, just as you do for a volley. But you tilt your racket face up, and you lift it as it meets the ball. That little lift, which should be executed with your whole arm and shoulder, is the tricky part. You have to learn by experience just how much oomph to put into it.

The lob-volley is a devastating weapon to use when you're at the net and your opposition wades in to shoot it out with you at pointblank range. If you send up one or two lob-volleys that drop just inside the baseline, you'll demoralize almost anybody. The surprise and shock are enough to unsettle even a good player because nobody will expect you to lob when you're in volleying position. After you've made a couple of these shots, the mere threat of them will keep your opponents from crowding the net.

Few of today's topflight players have enough finesse for this trick. Wayne Sabin used to bother everybody with it. Bobby Riggs and Pancho Segura could use it well. Few others have mastered it recently. However, that needn't discourage you from trying to learn it. Remember that it's much harder to make a lob-volley work in tournament tennis than in the middle-class game. Average players can't jump, smash, or cover court as the experts do. Nor can they make it so tough on a man who's at the net.

You'll have chances to try a lob-volley in ordinary play that you'd never have in first-class competition. And, if you get the knack, you'll score off your playmates with lob-volleys that would be murdered by the top-flighters. So you'll be smart to experiment with this shot, after you've gotten the rest of your arsenal in good working order.

Lift When You Lob

The plain lob is used both offensively and defensively in doubles, as you know by now, I trust. It should be used more than it is. Acquire a good one, and you'll keep most of your opponents falling over their own feet.

Learning to lob well is largely a matter of experience. Any dub can loft a ball into the air, but it's no cinch to make that ball land within a foot or so of the baseline. You acquire accuracy by constant trial and error. After a while you'll learn just about how hard to lift, from any place on the court, to put the ball where you want it. You can't aim a lob the way you can a drive or volley. But you can control it by regulating the speed of your racket's impact against the ball.

Your arm motion should be almost the same for a lob as for a drive. Stroke through the ball, but lift as you hit it. Then follow through with a rising arm. Easy does it. Keep your lob smooth, flowing, graceful.

Whenever your lobs aren't working well, concentrate on holding onto the ball longer with your racket. Feel the ball, just as you do for a drive. You need that solid feel, with the ball flattened against your racket for an appreciable instant. The cause of most errors in lobbing is stopping the racket too soon. Remember to follow through, and you'll probably be all right.

You've probably heard the phrase, "a fast lob." This doesn't mean that you speed up your movements when making a fast lob. It means that you send up a lob that drops more quickly so that your opponent hasn't time to run back and take it on the bounce. This kind of lob is used a lot as an offensive weapon against a net crowder. The high, slow lobs are defensive, to give a team time to get back into position after retrieving a hard shot. They're never outright point-winners. But a lob that goes up only nine or

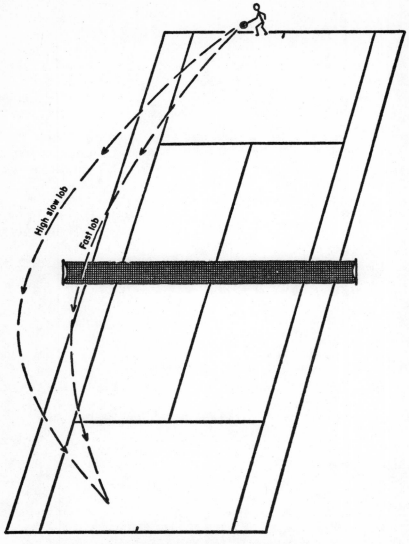

Figure 20. The lob: flight of the ball.

ten feet, scores cleanly or at least makes the enemy scramble wildly to get back a weak return.

The only difference in stroking, to make your lob a fast one, is that you lift it more gently. And probably you won't scoop it upward so sharply because you want a lower trajectory. (The harder you hit a lob, the more steeply you have to angle it upward, in order to make it drop in court.)

Keep trying all these different strokes. They're part of the equipment of the complete tennis player. The more you try them, the easier you'll find them.

Two-Fisted Shots

Until 1937 the tennis world never noticed any serious player using both hands simultaneously to swing a racket. Then along came a young Australian named John Bromwich who drove and volleyed from the forehand with both hands gripping the racket as if it were a baseball bat.

The bemused experts investigated, and discovered that the poor chap was a victim of bad habits formed in childhood. Starting at the age of six, he had learned by himself, using his father's racket. It was a good stout racket suited to the slow backcourt game his father played in New South Wales. Little John found it so heavy that he had to hold it with both hands in order to swing it with any joy or accuracy. But this came naturally, because he often played pickup games of cricket. So it was easy for him to hit his ragged tennis balls with a cricketer's grip and a cricket swing.

Before his father could get around to curing him of this atrocious unorthodoxy, John became the neighborhood champion, and his zany two-handed drive and volley seemed to work so well that nobody could talk him out of them. At seventeen he won the German singles championship from the great Baron Gottfried von Cramm; at eighteen he beat Don Budge in an exhibition in Australia; at nineteen in the Davis Cup challenge round he teamed with Adrian Quist to beat Budge and Mako in the doubles, then dusted off Bobby Riggs in the singles; at twenty he was ranked number two in the world.

He didn't hit the ball as hard as the average public playground player. How, then, could he win so often? Evidently his two-handed grip gave him a sharpshooter's accuracy. Ignoring his steadiness, some sports writers called Bromwich's style "childishly absurd . . . the world's most eccentric tennis game."

World War II cut off his chances to pile up a longer winning record. When he came back in 1946 he lost to Jack Kramer and Ted Schroeder, and they said afterward, "To make a double-handed shot you must take a half-step farther to the right, and then you have to take a half-step back to the left to get in position for the next shot. Those half-steps use a lot of energy in five sets. The percentages were against Brom."

Bromwich faded fast in the postwar years, and everyone concluded that his two-handed grip couldn't have been worth copying. But soon another eccentric player came along with a two-handed forehand which Kramer and many others freely admitted was "the best single shot in tennis." Pancho Segura from Ecuador was a bowlegged little man whose drives were as unerring as Bromwich's had been—and also a lot harder, because he moved forward and met the ball ahead of him.

Segura stayed near the top in pro tennis for twenty years, mainly because of his devastating double-handed drives. And yet, hardly anyone else experimented with two-fisted shots. Why? Well, because everyone assumed that Segura must be a freak. He had been a sickly kid, jeered at by playmates as "parrot foot." Because he was too small to swing the racket with one hand, he used both hands while secretly learning after hours at the Guayaquil tennis club where his father was caretaker. His crazy hay-pitching swing might be okay for him, the experts said, because the habit had become deep-rooted in childhood. But it would never work for anyone else.

People are slow to accept strange new ideas. Tennis is a century-old game, and its traditions were rigid for at least eighty of its years. The orthodox way of hitting a forehand drive remained the same because it had always been that way. Two-handed drives looked strange and awkward to nearly everyone who played the game.

However, little by little, the double grip ceased to be considered a freak shot. A few daring young tournament players began to use both hands to strengthen their forehand, or their backhand, or both. Some of them enjoyed phenomenal success. Chris Evert and her fiancé, Jimmy Connors, were considered to have the best backhand returns of service among American women and men; both used two-handed backhands. Two South African international stars, Cliff Drysdale and Drew McMillen, used two hands on their backhands—and McMillen also used two hands on all strokes, even volleys. He became, perhaps, the best men's doubles player of his time.

In the 1960s I discovered that a few of my pupils were able to correct bad forehands easily and quickly when I suggested that they try a two-handed grip, using their left hand either to hold their right wrist or to hold the lower part of the racket. This grip prevented them from flicking their wrist or poking the ball. They could scarcely avoid putting their whole body into a flowing stroke, as an expert does with his one-handed forehand. I realized that there was less that could go wrong. Other pupils having trouble with the backhand drive found that using both hands was a shortcut to improvement on that side, too.

So I had to reverse my opinion that a two-handed shot would require endless practice and would make the game harder for a spare-time player. I just hadn't experimented enough with it. When I did, I saw that many players found it less awkward than it looked. They said it did feel awkward at first in attempting running shots, but this soon smoothed out as players got used to it.

So now I suggest that you make some experiments of your own, perhaps against a practice wall. Try using your left hand (or wrist) to stiffen your right wrist and help guide your stroke, either on your forehand drive or your backhand or both. It's true, as Jack Kramer has always maintained, that you can't reach quite as far when your hands are together—but if you have to reach very far you'll probably make a poor shot anyhow, unless you're tournament caliber. For everyone except older players, whose habits are too firmly fixed to change, two-hand shots are well worth trying.

18 / Tennis Needn't Tire You

Are You Dying to Win?

Oleg Cassini, one of the members at my club, plays tennis so hard he has to go home to bed after a few sets. There are plenty of other members the same way. They play themselves to a standstill. They fight to the very last ounce of their strength, till their eyes are popping and their hearts are knocking their chests apart. Why? Because they want to win. Damn the torpedoes; to hell with the consequences; they're going to win if it kills them!

And sometimes it does. Almost every big tennis club has had one or two members drop dead on the courts. And it has plenty of others who died in bed, long before their time, because they didn't know when or how to ease up.

On the other hand, I know some smart old boys who can play on even terms with the average man of thirty-five or forty. These oldsters aren't supermen. They simply take tennis as a game, not a fight. They enjoy it. And they play well because they pace themselves well.

Sometimes I wonder about some of the highly successful businessmen I see around a tennis club. How much fun do they get out of life? They work at a terrific pace, with jitters and pounding all day long. Then they come out to the club and, instead of relaxing, they play tennis at the same terrific pace. Jitters and pounding every minute they're on the court. "I'm going to be a millionaire if it's the last thing I do," I've heard some of them say. So they get to be millionaires, and it's the last thing they do. "I'm going to be a good tennis player if it's the last thing I do," they also say. Well, I only hope they change their minds before it's too late.

Tennis shouldn't be a fight. It should be fun. Play it for pleasure, not to rub somebody else's face in the dirt, nor to show somebody you're still the powerhouse you were at eighteen.

The greatest danger in tennis, for men in their thirties and over, is their own competitive spirit. They still have that flaming urge to win in everything they try, and they can't control it. It finally consumes them. Too many Americans are old before their time just because they can't spare themselves, even slightly, in that big rat race to be a Great Success. They're smart enough to use their other assets wisely—their money, their real estate, their investments—but they throw away their most irreplaceable asset: their own bodies.

I hope you're the even smarter type who conserves himself as well as his possessions. You can do it, you know. You can have a grand time at tennis, win your share of matches, and still not wear yourself out.

Tennis at Fifty

Tennis, if you play it correctly, won't tire you any more than walking down the street. Maybe less. I'd get pretty tired if I had to walk the streets all day, but I can play tennis all day and never feel it.

The same is true of any other well-trained tennis player—or any expert at other sports, for that matter. A good athlete always looks effortless. Loose as ashes. Smooth and flowing as a dancer.

Tennis won't tire you if you loosen up and concentrate on being easy and rhythmic. Take your time, and use your head. Think about your form in every stroke. Make it smooth. You don't have to exert yourself in hitting a tennis ball.

A hard serve takes too much out of you. So does a slam-bang net-rushing game. So eliminate those tactics from your game, if you find yourself feeling as though you'd come out of a concrete mixer when you finish a set. Make your serve easy and graceful, and place it well. You can do plenty of damage that way—damage to your opponents, I mean. As for net sallies, you can still try them. Just plan them better. Work your way in more gradually. Instead of galloping in behind a flat drive, hit a lob or a high, slow drive that takes longer to reach your opponent, thereby giving you longer to move forward. Just jog into the forecourt—you'll have plenty of time.

Whether or not you can play good tennis in middle life depends pretty much on your mental attitude. What do you think about when you play? Are you fighting yourself every instant, exhorting yourself to do better, swearing at yourself when you miss one? Are you trying with might and main for every point? Thinking about the score, and the so-and-so on the other side of the net, and the lousy luck you're having?

If so, that's bad. Better change your thought patterns, or else give up tennis.

You should be thinking mainly about how you're stroking the ball, and secondly about the fun you're having. Keep your strokes smooth and relaxed, and keep happy. If you can do that, you'll be a good player for decades to come.

Allow a good margin of safety on your shots. Don't try to nick the corners. Don't try to skim the net. Give yourself a long, comfortable follow-through, with a slight lift as the ball leaves your racket to put some extra elevation on it. Take plenty of time on your shots, drawing your racket back early enough so that the whole stroke is one fluid movement.

When a player begins to simmer and boil internally, begins to feel the rage or desperation pounding in his temples and throat, then he tightens up. He flicks savagely at the ball, instead of stroking smoothly. He hits late. That's why the man who flogs himself into a frenzy on the court doesn't play good tennis.

He doesn't even run as well, when he tries to run hard. He lifts his knees high as he runs, pumping them up and down like pistons, which takes a lot out of him. Joe DiMaggio didn't run that way. Paavo Nurmi didn't. Tony Trabert didn't. Laver and Ashe don't.

They move fast, but they don't lift their feet high. They take long steps, gliding steps—low steps. Too hard work to pull the feet high off the ground is wasted energy. It's pushing your feet forward, not up, that makes you cover ground.

So give a little thought to the way you run when you're moving across the court in a hurry. Run low. Close to the ground. Loosen up your hips so you get a long, flowing stride. You won't get tired nearly so soon.

When to Turn on the Pressure

A smart player saves himself for the pinches. He coasts along when the point isn't important, then throws himself hard into a crucial point.

In every tennis match, certain points and certain games are much more important than others. Learn to recognize the "clutch" moments as they arise.

These are the times when you should go all out:

1. When the score is 40–30, or 30–40, or advantage. That's a tremendously big point. It means a whole game.

2. When you're serving and you're behind 15–30. Winning that point will put you on even terms. Losing it will mean you're very likely to have your service broken.

3. When you're serving and the game score is 4–5, or 5–6, or anything similar. Obviously, a service break means the set. Try to get the jump at the beginning of each of these critical games.

4. On the next point after a long rally. Have you ever noticed that, after an extended back-and-forth battle for one point, the next point is almost always a very short one? There's always a letdown. Somebody generally misses on the first or second shot. So, if you take great care to make a good shot or two on this point, you can be pretty sure that your opponent will blow.

5. On the next game after a long deuce game. The same principle applies here. When there's a protracted game, carried to deuce several times, a letdown follows and the next game is almost always short. Somebody falls apart temporarily. Don't let it be you. Bear down extra hard on that game, and you'll probably find it an easy one to win.

6. On the next game after a long deuce set. Those hard-fought sets that go to 8–6 or 9–7 leave both players limp. The beginning of the next set always seems an anticlimax. This is your big chance to catch your opponent while his guard is down. He won't be nearly as tough now as he was a moment ago, during the deuce set. Clench your teeth and go after him hard. You may get him on the run and take not just one but several games before he recovers. It often happens, even in tournaments.

On the other hand, there are certain stages in a match when it's silly to try hard for a point. The point just doesn't matter much. Here are the times when you should take life easy:

1.   When you're leading 40–love, or 40–15, or even 40–30. Why strain yourself to retrieve a tough shot now? Let it go. You still have plenty more chances to win the game.

2.   When your opponent's serving and you lead 3–5. It's idiotic to work hard to break his service again on this game. Your own serve is coming up. Wait for that game. It will be a much easier one to win, and you can run the set out at 6–4.

3.   When you're ahead by two sets, or even by one. The pressure is on him. He has to go all out to equalize. You can afford to save your strength while he's running himself into a lather. Just play normally as long as the set goes along on even terms, but don't run hard for any balls. And if the other man builds a lead, just keep the ball in play as much as you can, to make him run, without running yourself. Once you're behind, you'd be foolhardy to make an uphill fight to pull the set out of the fire.

4.   When you're ahead 4–1 in games. All you need is to win your next two service games, and you're in. But he's likely to feel desperate, and press hard, which probably will throw him off form and make things easier for you. Actually, 4–1 isn't such an enormous margin—it means only one service break—but it sounds terrible to the man who's on the short end of it. The psychological hazard often tightens him up. So you can lie back and wait for him to beat himself.

5.   When he's serving, and leads 40–0. Why exert yourself to win a hard point here? What good will it do you? You're not going to break his service once in a hundred times when he's this far ahead, so take it easy.

Some players fight fiercely for every point, regardless of the score. They're dumb. They waste a lot of their strength on unimportant points, which leaves them less for the important ones.

Another important thing is to know when to walk off the court. Most men play too long at one session. If you're half dead after three sets, use some common sense! Hold yourself to two sets in the future. And if you begin to feel disturbing palpitations and hot flushes in the middle of a set—or if you're in trouble from nothing more serious than that your feet are killing you—don't be afraid to walk off the court in the middle of a set. The greatest tournament stars have done it, in the greatest tournaments.

Call for a rest, or call the match off. It's better to default a match than to wind up in a doctor's care. Nobody with an ounce of brains is going to resent it if you stop play during a match. Just explain that you're not feeling well. Enough said, among gentlemen.

Pick Some Pushovers

If you've reached the age of discretion, you'll want to spend some of your tennis time with weaker players. They're good for you. They make it possible for you to smooth out strokes, to get a good workout, to keep yourself in condition. Your big matches with players your own caliber will be easier for you if you've spent some time conditioning yourself against somewhat inferior sparring partners.

Few people realize how much benefit they can get from a session with a poorer player. They play their usual game, win easily, and an insipid time is had by all. They don't realize that a game with a weak opponent is their big chance to improve their own weak spots.

When you're playing someone you know you can beat, feed his strong points. Give him the shots he can make best. Place your serve where he can handle it easiest. Remember, you want rallies, not quick points.

If your opponent has some glaring weakness, keep away from it. At the same time, expose your own weaknesses. If your backhand is wobbly, run around the balls to take them on your backhand. If you're a baseline player, take the net at every chance. If you're a specialist at volleying, don't take the net at all; concentrate on building up your baseline game.

Fred Perry, Wimbledon champion in '34, '35 and '36, rarely won a practice match. He knew that practice was the time to take risks. That's one of the reasons he became the greatest player of his time. Every day he strengthened his game, even when he could find only a mediocre opponent. He always played the difficult shot in preference to the easy one, kept away from his good shots and polished his poor ones. It paid off.

Sharpen up your accuracy when you're playing with someone who can't give you a tussle. Pick out certain spots on the court, and see how close to those spots you can put the ball. Only don't select spots near the sidelines. Aim at targets which your pushover opponent can reach easily.

Try to place the ball exactly where he can handle it the best. The better you learn to control the ball, the easier you'll be able to dust the lines when you get into a tough match. You get many more chances to work on accuracy against a weak opponent than against a strong one.

A poor player is always grateful for a chance to tackle a stronger one. It makes him extend himself and thereby improves his game. So why not invite some third-rater to play you, every now and then? He can make you extend yourself too, now that you know the trick of aiming at his strength and exposing your own weakness.

Another good way to keep from tiring yourself too much at tennis is to play less singles, more doubles. Top-speed doubles can be a killing game, but you needn't play at top speed. If you've studied the chapters on doubles strategy, you know how to manipulate the game to save your legs. Keep practicing until you've mastered the art of serving easily and sauntering to the net. It's all a matter of placing your serve well, taking two steps forward and handling the return of service from there, then moving the rest of the way to the forecourt behind your first drive. Many men are good doubles players at fifty or sixty. They know how to jockey the play, slow it down when necessary, and save their strength for the crucial spots. You can do the same!

19 / The Left-Handed Player

Those Sinister Serves

"Sinister" originally meant left-handed. You can understand why if you've ever gone up against a left-handed tennis player. A southpaw is about as harmless an opponent as Dr. Fu Manchu. Be prepared for nothing but trouble when you tackle one.

Practically every left-hander has an especially sinister weapon—sinister in every sense of the word—in his serve. A good left-handed serve is a much hotter potato to handle than a good right-handed serve. Why? Because it breaks in the opposite direction from the serves you've been used to.

When a right-hander sends an American twist serve at you, it always bounces to your left. So if you've played against opponents who use the twist, probably you've developed a reflex. You automatically set yourself to make a backhand return whenever you see somebody arch himself backward in that unmistakable American twist windup. But now, against a left-hander with a twist serve, your reflex crosses you up. When his serve hits, it bounces away in the wrong direction—to your right, instead of to your left as you've learned to expect. Theoretically his twist should be easier to handle than a right-hander's because you take it on your forehand. But actually, if you've developed a normal set of tennis habits, you'll find yourself making the wrong move every time that twist starts across the net toward you.

It's even worse for you when a left-hander gives you the more common type of serve, the slice. A right-hander's slice slides off to your right. But a portsider's slice veers to your left. Better watch yourself, or his serve will have you whirling like an egg beater. Not only does it attack you on your weaker side, but it attacks you unexpectedly, because in years of tennis playing you've always been accustomed to seeing that serve shoot toward your forehand after it hits.

If you've ever watched Rod Laver, the Australian internationalist, hammer his opponents cross-eyed with his southpaw serves, you know how tough a really hard-hitting left-hander can be. Or if you remember back to the days when Johnny Doeg was national champion, you have an even more vivid idea. Doeg was a huge, brawny kid with a left-handed serve that landed like a pile driver. He didn't have much else, but it was enough. Even Bill Tilden and Frank Shields couldn't get geared up to break his serve when he was in his prime.

Since left-handed serves have wreaked such havoc in the world's top tennis circles, you can imagine that they'll make trouble in your own league too. Any time you square off against a southpaw, even if he's just an average player, beware of his serves!

Reverse Your Game

Most tennis addicts who use their brains when they play have always cultivated the habit of hitting to their opponents' backhand. It's just horse sense. Nine out of ten players below the tournament class are weaker on that side. So every thoughtful strategist tries to hit most of his own forehand shots down the line, and his backhands cross-court, in order to keep the ball on the other fellow's left. He probably does this so persistently that it becomes an ingrained habit over the years. He does it almost without thinking.

Which means that he's simply playing Santa Claus to a left-handed opponent. Give a left-hander a ball on his left, and of course you're giving him a forehand shot. This happens to be exactly what he wants. Above everything else, he's probably anxious to keep the ball off his backhand. For some reason, nearly every southpaw has a weaker backhand but a stronger-than-average forehand.

Maybe this is because southpaws get more forehand shots and fewer backhand ones than the rest of us do. We're all used to aiming our drives and volleys into our opponents' left-hand court, and we can't break the habit. So a left-hander receives a steady stream of balls on his forehand, while right-handers have to keep taking shots on their backhand or else running around them. The portsider doesn't have to worry much about running around backhand shots. Practically nothing comes to his backhand!

If you want to beat a good left-hander, you'll have to think about what you're doing every second. You'll have to go counter to all your instincts and keep aiming the ball at the other half of the court than you normally do. Try to hit cross-court on all your forehand shots, and straight down the line on all your backhands. This sounds easy. But you may find that in actuality it reduces your game to a grand snafu. You probably don't realize how seldom you've deliberately aimed at your opponent's right-hand sectors. It will seem awkward and unnatural, especially on your drives. You'll have to concentrate, instead of just letting your shots flow through their normal patterns. But if you make yourself do it, you'll find it works beautifully. It's the only smart way to play to a left-hander—unless he happens to be a prodigy with a good backhand, and there aren't very many of those.

So it's a pretty safe rule to reverse your game when you tangle with a southpaw. Keep putting the ball to his right instead of his left. And when he's serving, expect the ball to bounce in the opposite direction from which it normally would.

Reverse your own service, too. You're probably so used to aiming at the opposition's backhand corner, even with your slice serve, that you'll go slightly insane trying to change. But you can get the hang of it if you put your mind to the problem. After all, your slice serve naturally tends to angle off toward the receiver's right. Just let it do what comes naturally, for a change. Accentuate it. Let it go more to the right, instead of trying to make it go less. The farther to the right you can put it, against a left-hander, the harder time he'll have running around it.

Look, No Forehands!

The problem of where to put a left-handed doubles partner is a perplexing one. If you have him play the left half of the court, then all the balls which pour through the center will be on both your backhand and his. But if you take the left side, and put him on the right, then you'll have two forehands to use against the center shots and nothing but backhands for the balls in both alleys.

After long thought and fervent prayer, I've finally come to the conclusion that it's better to put a lefty on the left half of the court, if both partners are about equal in ability. This arrangement generally gives the team less grief, in club doubles, and it's the line-up always used in hot-shot tournament doubles. Johnny Doeg always played the left side of the court, even when Tilden was his partner. Rod Laver, the leading left-hander of today's tennis, always takes the left side. So does Roger Taylor.

Of course most balls go into the middle, in doubles, and it may seem suicidal to have no forehand there to cope with them. But the right-handed partner may have an adequate backhand, or the left-hander may be able to run around many of those center shots and hit them with his forehand. Remember that it's much easier to run around a ball that's coming down the middle than it is to run around one that's angling off to the side. Anybody who tries to get outside a ball that lands in the alley is leaving himself as wide open as a house with a wall gone.

That's why the left-hander ought to play the left half. No forehands in the middle are better than no forehands on the alleys. Even though there aren't as many balls in the alleys, a weak backhand there is more disastrous than in the center.

However, if you're teamed with a lefty who is markedly weaker than you are, forget about this rule and take the left side yourself, just as you would with a weak right-handed teammate. Whether a player hits from port or starboard, if he's a definite drawback to the team he can be kept out of harm's way more easily on the right half of the court.

Doubles Against a Southpaw

If you're in a doubles match and the left-hander is on the other team, playing in his own left half as he should, then you and your partner ought to fire everything down the center. Work on those two backhands. Of course, if the other partner happens to have an unusually strong backhand, this wouldn't be such shrewd strategy, and you'd better start probing for some other weakness. Ordinarily, though, this won't happen. Hit to the center and rush the net, if you want to win against most pairs that include a southpaw.

If the opposition is silly enough to put the left-hander on the right, just keep feeding the ball into his alley and watch him suffer. You can do this anyway, during half of each game when his team is serving. Then the partners must change sides on every serve, and you can really run him ragged on his backhand.

Another thing to remember, against a left-handed doubles player, is that he's likely to be wicked with a short forehand cross-court. The average right-hander is pretty sloppy when he tries to take a shallow ball on his forehand. He can't put it cross-court at all. But the average left-hander is sure death on such balls, for some mysterious reason. Lefties have a sort of topspin drive on their forehand that makes it easy for them to race in on a shallow ball and whip it over the net low and hard. Try not to give them these chances.

Take full advantage of a southpaw's weak backhand. You can capitalize on it better in doubles than you can in singles. Just move into the forecourt every time you make him try a backhand shot. Watch for other weaknesses, too, and take the net whenever you play those weaknesses.

If You're Left-Handed

Speaking now to lefties themselves, I'd like to remind you first of all that the other chapters in this book are written just as much for you as for right-handers. Everything we've covered in the fields of strategy, psychology, conditioning, equipment, and the like applies to you. As for the chapters on strokes, they'll work just as well for you as for anyone else, if you just read "left" for "right" whenever it occurs in the text. Simply reverse the sides, and you can use exactly the same motions and footwork that any right-hander does.

The chapter you ought to read with your racket in hand, standing in front of a mirror, is the one on backhands. If you're like nearly all south-side players, your backhand is your big weakness. Work on it. Make chances to use it. Whenever you're playing someone you know you can beat, take every possible shot on your backhand. Run around the ball if necessary to get it on your right. Get rid of that weakness!

Whenever you use your forehand, try to hit it cross-court so you'll be putting the ball on your opponent's backhand. By the same token, you ought to make your backhanders straight down the line, rather than diagonal, so they'll force your opponent to hit off his weaker side—his left.

In serving, cultivate your slice serve. Work to put more and more sidespin on it. The slice serve is the left-hander's deadliest weapon. It always breaks to his opponent's backhand, which is a nasty surprise for the guy it happens to. Make your break as sharply as possible—and train yourself to charge the net behind your serve, because you're going to get lots of weak returns from that slice of yours, and you can put them away for quick points if you grab the net in time. As you run in, after serving on the odd points, run diagonally to your right, rather than straight ahead toward the net. This is because the puny backhand returns of your serve will almost always float into the right-hand side of your court.

As you've probably gathered in reading this chapter, you have a definite edge over right-handed players of your own class. As long as they fail to solve your service, and don't get smart enough to start pounding your backhand, you'll probably beat them. However, why sit back and wait for them to wise up? Keep the jump on them. Make your slice sharper and sharper—shore up your weak backhand—learn to aim every shot to take advantage of enemy flaws—and maybe you'll never be beaten!

20 / Women's Singles and Doubles

Shall We Join the Ladies?

There ought to be at least one chapter in this book devoted strictly to women's tennis. This is it.

However, this isn't the only chapter that ladies are allowed to read. Mesdames et mademoiselles, if you're interested in tennis I hope you've been with us all along. The earlier chapters are for you too. A woman should hit her forehand or backhand the same way a man does. The basic principles of strategy are the same for either sex. Just read "she" instead of "he" in most of the sentences in this book, and they still make sense.

This chapter is a sort of postgraduate course for the ladies—or for the gentleman who wants to give a few special tips to his wife, daughter, or girl friend. This is where we take up the fine points of the ladies' game—the small differences that can make a big difference.

Incidentally, it's much easier for a woman to become a good player than it is for a man. A feminine beginner can get all kinds of advice, coaching, and practice from the best men players who happen to be around. A man is just naturally chivalrous when it comes to helping the opposite sex learn tennis. But will he help another member of his own sex? Haw!

So take heart, you ladies who fear you'll never be much good at the game. Just wander out to the tennis courts, every day you have a little spare time, and scatter a few hints among your gentlemen acquaintances who play well. They'll practice with you. They'll point out your weaknesses (and please remember not to feel hurt when they do; it's your strokes they're criticizing, not you) and help you correct them. They'll give you the constant coaching and exercise that anybody of either sex needs in order to become a presentable player. A male beginner wouldn't dare ask good players to work out with him, and probably would get a polite straight arm if he did dare. But you can ask, and receive.

Incidentally, it's interesting to note that galleries have grown steadily for singles matches between good women players. This isn't entirely due to the fact that nationwide interest in tennis has grown phenomenally. Nor is it altogether due to the beauty, charm, and grace of so many feminine stars in recent years. There's also another reason for those crowded grandstands.

The women haven't concentrated on the big serve-and-rush game, and practically all male stars have ever since Jack Kramer and Ted Schroeder perfected it in 1946. When women approach the net, they usually do so behind an artfully placed stroke that draws an opponent out of position, rather than behind a bullet serve. This makes for more interesting maneuvers and jockeying—a game with which most spectators can identify, since it's the style they themselves usually strive for. Few tennis buffs can afford the hours of daily practice needed to develop a power serve and quick-kill style—and besides, it's essentially dull. As Kramer himself wrote in 1972 in *The Fireside Book of Tennis*, "The public does not yet understand the serve-and-volley game. It's boring. Someone serves, comes into net, and either makes a good volley or forces an error. There are no back-court maneuvers; the ground stroke artists don't win. . . . I sincerely believe something should be done as the game is becoming less and less attractive to the spectators."

This isn't true of women's tennis. It is becoming more and more attractive to the spectators of both sexes. Watching it, they see strategy and strokes that they can use in their own game. If you haven't watched any top-grade women's tennis, I'd suggest you do so. You'll enjoy it.

On Guard!

As we noted in the chapter on mixed doubles, women, in general, have had less intensive athletic training and practice than most men. As a result, certain mistakes crop up commonly among run-of-the-club women players.

So—speaking now to feminine readers—let me warn you about these mistakes. Concentrate on correcting them and you'll be a much better player than the average.

First of all, beware of favoring your forehand too much, at the expense of your backhand. This is the besetting sin of most women players, even the champions. May Sutton Bundy, one of the great women stars of all time, won Wimbledon without any semblance of a backhand. She'd run clear outside the court, across her backhand alley, in order to take a ball on her forehand. Then she could sprint all the way across the court, in those billowing ankle-length skirts of the day, in time to retrieve a return to the opposite corner. She won because she was fast as a gazelle. Most women aren't nearly that fast and can be beaten easily by anyone who keeps putting the ball on their backhand. Get yourself into a different category. Become one of the few girls who know what to do about a ball on their left. It isn't terribly hard to develop a smooth, easy backhand stroke—see Chapter 7—and it will immediately put you among the elite of feminine players.

Here's another mistake to watch out for: Don't hang back around the baseline too much. It's too easy to build up a phobia against net play unless you take yourself in hand.

The first few times you venture into the forecourt and see those balls come whizzing at you from close range, you may be frightened nigh unto death. But don't weaken. Keep going to the net. Familiarity breeds contempt. In a surprisingly short time you'll get used to taking the ball on the fly, and it won't bother you a bit. In fact, you'll find that it's great fun.

Maybe you're wondering if you won't get maimed, particularly when you're a green player, by those point-blank shots you face at the net. It almost never happens. In the first place, whether you're trained or untrained, you have instinctive reflexes that protect you. You throw up an arm or you dodge or duck without even thinking when something comes at you unexpectedly. I've been around tennis courts practically all my life, and I have yet to see anybody get hit hard enough by a tennis ball to feel hurt for more than a minute or two.

You'll almost immediately develop the habit of holding your racket up in front of you and using it automatically to block off balls headed your way. This starts as a defense mechanism, but before long it develops into an offensive weapon. The mere act of blocking off a ball at the net often wins a point for you. Pretty soon you'll be pouncing on balls, instead of warding them off. You'll have a net game!

A woman with a net game is everybody's sweetheart. She's much in demand for mixed doubles, for women's doubles, and even for singles practice against a man. Furthermore, she'll be able to beat quite a few men.

There are lots of men around every tennis club who are strictly chop-stroke artists. They slice and undercut every ball. A woman who goes to the net can murder them. You see, a chop is rising as it comes across the net. You need only put your racket in front of it and it plops dead in your opponent's forecourt. When you're at the net you're supposed to aim every shot downward—and you just can't help hitting it down when the ball is rising as it comes to you.

On the other hand, I've seen several friendly matches between a woman who had beautiful smooth sweeping ground strokes and a man who had a jerky chopping game. The woman should have won easily. But she would never take the net so she couldn't put the ball away. The man just kept chopping the ball back until she finally made an error. If she had only moved in to volley his chop shots, she would have made him look very sick indeed. Instead she stayed back, and got beaten.

With a good volley and a good backhand, you'll be the class of your own league. Work on those two shots!

Many women (and quite a few men, when they start) tend to be too tense. They jerk and flick and poke at the ball instead of handling themselves as gracefully as women do elsewhere. They try too hard because they're nervous.

Watch yourself for symptoms of nervousness. If you feel them coming on, slow down. Take long, deep breaths. At the start of each point, stroll into position instead of bustling. Think about one or two of your muscles, and relax them. Then think of other muscles, and relax those. Get yourself thoroughly loosened up.

Most important of all, think about a long follow-through for each stroke. Make it flow—long and easy and graceful. Start drawing your racket back sooner than usual to give yourself plenty of time. Then take a smooth stroke, and follow through all the way. No pushball. Remember to stroke *through* the ball, not at it. Keep it on your racket longer as you hit so you get that solid feel all through your hand and wrist and forearm.

If you keep thinking about these things, concentrating on smooth easy form as you hit each ball, you'll have no time to think about being nervous. Try it and see if I'm not right!

Women's Doubles

If you play doubles to win, then take the net. That's where points are won. Even if your partner won't go up there with you, go up alone. One player at the net is better than none.

It's always better, of course, if both members of the team come up to the net together. It puts the opposition at a disadvantage. You're up there on top of them, in a solid, unbroken front. Wherever they drive the ball, you or your partner stand ready to cut it off. If they remember that the best answer to a net game is lobbing, you're still not likely to have much trouble because it takes a polished player to lob well. You'll probably get mostly shallow lobs that you can reach by retreating only a couple of steps. Don't try to smash those lobs, unless you're powerfully muscled. Instead, just take aim and place the ball neatly and smoothly to one side, where they'll have to run like mad to retrieve it. Then step in close to the net again, because their return is sure to be weak, and you can put it away for an ace.

If you and your partner both dislike playing in the forecourt, then your best chance of winning is to mix up your opponents with a change of pace, an unpredictable variety of shots. Feed one of the opposing women a short ball that makes her run up to the net, then lob over her head. Send over a long drive, then a short one, then a diagonal one. Aim first into one alley and then the other.

If your opponents rush the net, don't try for a passing shot. Loft a skyscraper ball over their heads. In fact, once you acquire the knack of lobbing fairly deep, you ought to compel your opponents to come to the net, so you can chase them back again with a lob. That business of racing up-and-back, up-and-back time after time is not only exhausting but discouraging.

Who is the better player, you or your partner? Whoever it is, she ought to play in the backhand half of the court—the left half—when your team is receiving service. This is the same principle that knowledgeable men's doubles teams use. The stronger player always takes the backhand half. This is because the player on that side gets more chances at forehand shots that can be clean winners. Inexperienced players don't understand this. But it pays off in extra points so make sure that you and your partner always follow this system. If you want a more detailed explanation of why the system is important, see Chapter 14.

In mixed doubles, if the lady possesses the weaker shot then she should play the righthand side, the forehand, in receiving service. Let the man do the smashing. But don't stand back and assume that he wants to cover the whole court. Some women tend to be timid. They think the man will be annoyed if they reach for a shot and make an error. Quit worrying and get in the game! Whether or not your partner is a better player than you are, he wants you to have your share of the fun. He doesn't expect you to hit every shot perfectly; all players make some clumsy errors. So step in and try for every ball in your sector. He'll like it much better that way, unless he's one of those rare ball hogs, and you never need play with a ball hog more than once.

Of course, when you're playing mixed doubles in a tournament, or in a redhot grudge fight, then sharing the fun becomes unimportant. If your partner is a better player than you are, tell him you want him to take every ball he can possibly reach. You stand close to the net, and hit only the balls that come to you. Let him take everything else. This way you maximize your chances of beating the other team.

Losing? Get Smart!

When the battle goes against you, either in doubles or singles, your normal human tendency will be to tighten up. Don't. Relax, and put your brains to work. Why are you losing? What are you doing wrong?

Maybe you're hitting most balls over the line. If so, you're hitting too hard. Stop trying to whale the stuffing out of the ball.

Maybe you're hitting your shots short, popping them into the net. This means you're poking at the ball. The way to overcome it is to think about your follow-through. Swing your racket in a long, fluid stroke through the path of the ball, and you'll find yourself making fewer errors.

Another possible cause of hitting short is standing too far back to receive service. Maybe you ought to move in a little closer. Try it and see if it helps. Also move in anyway for the second service if the first is a fault because you know there's a softer ball coming.

If you seem to be splattering your shots outside in all directions, just slow down and concentrate on stroking the ball back into the middle of the court. Play safe. Don't try to place the ball, nor blast it, nor maneuver your opponent out of position. Just keep getting the ball back, with medium length and medium speed, squarely down the middle. After a while you'll steady down and you'll be able to hit a few fancy licks again.

Meanwhile you also should be giving thought to your opponent and her weaknesses. What are they? What kind of shots bother her? Shots to her backhand, probably. Give her plenty of them. And give her plenty of lobs. Girls who haven't practiced a lot are likely to have a weak overhead game. You can pull yourself out of a pretty deep hole if you'll just keep lobbing and keep putting the ball on your opponent's backhand.

Advice to Advisers

Now we turn to the gentlemen again. This next section is addressed to any man who is teaching tennis to a woman, of whatever age.

First of all, remember that the younger your pupil is, the better. If you have a daughter, you can start her playing tennis at age nine or younger. Even when she's just a toddler, play catch with her whenever you can, to tune up her reflexes, and get her skipping rope as often as possible to give her strong legs and make her fast on her feet.

When you begin teaching a woman, take her background into consideration. If she hasn't spent a lot of time in athletics, she's unlikely to be especially strong or well-coordinated. But she'll improve if you keep encouraging her. Don't be annoyed if she has no timing at first, if she hits the ball on the wooden edge of the racket, or misses it completely. This is to be expected. So don't get discouraged, and don't let your pupil get discouraged. Remind her that every learner has to pass through this awkward stage and that she'll emerge from it soon.

The first thing to teach her is the proper grip (see Chapter 4). Then show her the forehand drive, and begin rallying with her. Next teach her how to serve.

With this elementary equipment, she can go out right away and begin playing. A serve and a drive are the only essentials. In the second or third lesson, start teaching her the backhand—and also introduce her to net play. It's easier to learn to volley early than it is later on, when she may have developed a habit of staying in the back court.

Keep rallying with her. Informal rallying is better than a formal game with score being kept because she can relax and play more joyously when it doesn't count. But make sure that she uses her backhand and her volleys during this informal sparring.

Never criticize her, except indirectly. It's human nature to resent criticism. Instead of saying, "Don't do this," say, "Do that." Advocate "a little more" of something. Say, "You're doing fine! Now just change slightly this way, and you'll make it even better."

Whenever she makes a shot that is good, considering her present stage of development, comment enthusiastically; she deserves it. Look for things to praise. She'll probably realize that you're using standard coaching psychology on her, but she'll still like it better that way. I never saw anyone yet, male or female, who wasn't pleased by a well-placed compliment.

21 / Tennis Elbow, Tennis Toe and Other Troubles

Your Aching Elbow

"There are at least eleven specific elbow complaints that have been called 'tennis elbow,' " Dr. Robert P. Nirschi wrote in a tennis magazine.

Any recurring pain on the outer side of the elbow is likely to be labeled a tennis elbow when tennis players suffer from it. Golfers complain of golf elbow, which seems to be the same kind of pain. Baseball pitchers tend to get a "sore arm," which is a sore elbow as often as not. Likewise there are plenty of people who play no games but nevertheless are suddenly afflicted with lameness or ache in that same pesky joint of the right arm. (Only lefthanders seem to get a sore left elbow.)

One friend of mine, a deskbound business man, decided to try to build muscle by raising and lowering his heavy briefcase as he walked from parking lot to office building each morning. This should have accomplished what he wanted, since it's basically a standard exercise done with a dumbbell. But on the fourth morning his elbow suddenly got so sore that it ached all day, kept him awake for several nights, and for weeks afterward gave him sharp pain whenever he tried to lift a teapot or reach out for a handshake. Evidently he'd slightly twisted his elbow each time he lifted the briefcase in midstride, and consequently had torn some fibers of the muscle attached to the elbow bone. This is approximately the same mishap that befalls a tennis player when he or she gets tennis elbow.

Torn fibers or ligaments are what hurt when you get an aching elbow from tennis. Unlike the shoulder joint and the hip joint, which can swivel in any direction within certain limits, the elbow joint is a hinge that moves freely in only one direction. It has a special arrangement of ligaments by which the radius and ulna, the two bones of the lower arm, can be twisted to cross over each other. This gives the lower arm some flexibility—but not quite enough flexibility for the strains and twists to which it is sometimes subjected by a tennis player with bad habits of stroking or serving.

When you put too much wrist into a shot, you're almost sure to roll your forearm over sharply. I explained in earlier chapters that you should hit the ball smack in the center of your racket, stroking through the ball with a locked wrist. When you twist or snap your wrist, you're not only savaging the fibers of the muscle attached to your elbow bone but also hitting a bad shot.

Where does the power come from in your strokes? If you're a good player, it usually comes from your shoulders and hips. But if you're inexperienced or poorly trained, you probably use your forearm to get whatever power you muster. You flick, swat, or jerk. This tears those vulnerable fibers and ligaments on the outer side of your elbow.

How about your serve? If your arm stops suddenly after you hit the ball, something twists and gives. A full follow-through protects your elbow.

Each shot that twists your elbow may strain more fibers. Usually a cumulative effect brings on the pain later, rather than at the instant you tear any given fiber. If you play again soon in the hope that the pain will cure itself, more bad strokes may form nonelastic scar tissue in the elbow. This scar tissue often tears repeatedly, with worse pain.

So now you know: Usually the cure for tennis elbow is to cure whatever stroke twists your elbow. Go back and review the chapters on forehand, backhand, and service. Then look up the last section of Chapter 17, which tells about two-handed forehand and backhand strokes. If you'll just use your left hand and arm to help guide your racket and stiffen your right wrist (or vice versa if you're a lefty) there'll be less strain on your elbow and the ache may disappear rather soon.

When you're serving with a sore elbow, toss the ball more to the side, and slice it. (Probably you already do this on your second serves, if you've taken my advice in Chapter 5, but you can slice your first serves too to spare your elbow.) A slicing stroke on a volley will help too, because you'll turn your hand up as you make the shot, thus avoiding the wrenching roll of the forearm. Just remember to punch the ball with locked elbow and wrist.

If you keep these points in mind, the dreaded warning from doctors, "Better lay off tennis awhile," needn't apply. You can play with an aching elbow if you use slices and flowing two-handed shots, or if you smooth out your strokes by other means.

There are extra measures you can take, too, to avoid a recurrence or to minimize pain from a yet uncured tennis elbow. One is to lengthen your warmup; take an extra ten- or fifteen-minutes' exercise before you start to play. Warmed ligaments will stretch without tearing. So practice some arm-swinging exercises for a time without the racket, then swing your racket another few minutes without hitting the ball. With and without the racket, concentrate on good form, stroking smoothly, swinging your hips and shoulders loosely, keeping your wrist locked, following through all the way.

You can also switch to a lighter racket. If you've been using a heavy big-throated wooden racket, you've probably been aggravating the miseries in your elbow. Try one of the newer wood frames with thin throat design, or a steel or aluminum racket.

Maybe you can even switch to lighter balls. The heavy-duty and/or rubber-center balls now so popular (because they last longer) actually do weigh more, and can make your poor elbow feel as if you've struck solid lead when you stroke awkwardly. The regular pressure-packed "championship" balls, or even some old worn-out balls, if you're just practicing, will take less effort and therefore put less strain on your elbow during a bad shot.

After playing, if your elbow aches and especially if it's swollen, put an icebag on it or put it in a pail of ice water until the ache disappears and the swelling goes down. For less painful cases, heat in any form will usually help by increasing blood supply in the elbow. Doctors also recommend massage with a methyl-salicylate liniment. Athletic trainers sometimes use ultrasound in low frequencies, but never longer than three minutes. Too long a treatment, or too high a frequency, can cause bone damage.

What about a cortisone shot? It can ease the pain. But the pain will return if you continue to do something wrong when you hit tennis balls. Cortisone is usually prescribed only if other treatment fails, because it sometimes causes unpleasant side effects such as fidgetiness during the day and insomnia at night.

Surgery? Only if the alternative is to give up tennis. Chronic tennis elbow might—in rare cases—be a form of bursitis (fluid or calcium deposits in the joint where a tendon and bone come together) or some other unusual abnormality. Remember that any of eleven different complaints can make your elbow ache. Some of these can be successfully treated by a simple surgical operation to change whatever is abnormal in your elbow. But I'd guess that of every hundred cases of tennis elbow, only one or two call for surgery. The others can be cured by improving your stroke and taking a few of the supplementary measures I've just mentioned.

Tender Care for Foot Faults

W. C. Fields used to complain that if he said he had hurt his foot he got sympathy, but if he said his feet hurt all he got was a laugh.

Tennis players whose feet hurt now avoid laughter by explaining that they suffer from "tennis toe." This is a new malady that has recently stricken several parts of the country, although I have yet to hear of it on the Pacific Coast where I teach.

Tennis toe can sometimes be painful enough to make walking difficult, despite the small size of the distressed area. The trouble starts with rupture of blood vessels under the toenail, usually in the big toe. The damaged vessels turn an alarming purple. Sometimes there is swelling in addition to pain.

What causes tennis toe? Experts disagree.

I've seen published statements that it is most likely to occur on cement and other hard-surface courts. Supposedly, the new high-traction tennis shoes can bring a player to a sudden stop on a hard surface, jamming his toes against the tough and unyielding front of the shoe. I can't believe this theory, because I've never heard of a case among California players, and cement courts are almost universal in California.

Here are a couple of guesses of my own. Softer courts, like clay, let the foot slide more, and perhaps friction between the toenail and the top of the tough shoe could cause these blood blisters. Or perhaps in the hotter summers east of the Rockies tennis players' feet tend to swell more, making their shoes tighter and putting pressure on big toenails. (It's a fact that all feet do swell slightly during a long hike or a long tennis match.)

These are the only suppositions that can account for the number of wails from eastern and southern tennis clubs, where clay courts are common and so is tennis toe.

I certainly am not an expert on this new affliction, since I've met only a few players (easterners) who've ever mentioned it. But I do know that blistered feet have always been more common on clay courts, and tennis toe is basically a blood blister, so it might arise from similar causes.

Anyhow, what can be done about it?

Dr. Lionel Goldstein, the tennis-playing president of a podiatry association in Miami, Florida, says the injury can be partially prevented "by cutting the toenails fairly short and wearing cotton socks that will soften the impact of the toes on the shoe."

Dr. Harold V. Roth, a Los Angeles foot specialist, cautions against the new European-designed tennis shoes. "They provide better traction," he says, "but they also aggravate the tennis toe condition because the longer and narrower toe sections crowd the big toe, compressing it sideways and on top." The new shoes have leather or tough synthetic rubber toe sections which don't give as much as the older, less durable sneakers.

Certainly the problem never arose in the old days when we all wore the familiar canvas sneakers. They were light and flimsy enough so that the big toe could bulge through the front of the sneaker instead of being compressed too painfully.

When you buy tennis shoes, make sure they're not too short. Press your finger down in front, to see if there's enough room there to avoid pressure during sudden stops.

You might also try wearing two pairs of socks, as advised by experienced long-distance walkers and hikers: a thin inner pair and a thick outer pair of textured cotton or wool. The inner pair acts as a second skin and takes the friction, of which there is bound to be some during vigorous tennis even in the best-fitting shoes. This precaution also helps prevent blisters. Furthermore the air space between socks insulates your feet, on the thermos-bottle principle, to keep them at normal temperature instead of overheating.

I suspect that most complaints of tennis toe and blistered feet come from people who play six or eight hours of tennis in one day after a week or more spent mostly sitting down. Feet get tender if they aren't toughened a little by frequent exercise. Maybe you should condition them by soaking them in brine, as marathoners do. Or maybe you should merely start your tennis more gradually, in shorter sessions.

Painful feet, like a tired body, are comforted at the end of a long tennis match by a good soaking in warm—not hot—water. (If the skin or toenails are tender, hot water will only make them more so.) A cool rinse, careful drying, a dusting of talcum powder, and a rest with the feet raised on a pillow—so there'll be less blood in them—will usually relieve sore toes as well as aching foot muscles and burning blisters. You should also put a Band-Aid over a blister, as you probably know.

Keeping Fit After Forty

As we grow older, most of us grow more vulnerable to various aches and pains, especially if our exercise comes only at intervals of a week or longer.

Older people feel the hot weather more now than they did as young-sters. If they play tennis in the hot sun they're more likely to get head-aches and possibly severe sunstroke—unless they wear headgear of some kind to protect their heads and drink enough liquid between games to keep from getting thirsty.

They're more likely to get a muscle pull—which comes from a quick lunge in an unexpected direction—unless they take time to warm up thoroughly before they play, especially on a chilly day.

Likewise, too brief a warmup can leave them susceptible to "tennis leg," as it's called in the 1969 edition of McGraw-Hill's *Emergency Medical Guide*: "a tear in the Achilles tendon at the back of the heel, or in the big muscle that forms the calf of the leg (in which case it's the same 'charlie horse' known to football and track athletes)." If you feel sudden sharp pains anywhere in your leg, better hobble off the court and find an icebag for the painful area; then take some aspirin or whatever usually works best for you in quieting pain. If the pang is still bad next day, better see a doctor and get the muscle taped up.

Tendonitis, like tennis elbow, can be brought on by awkward jerky swings of a tennis racket. Ditto for a sprained or strained wrist, especially when a server puts a lot of wrist-snap into his serve. But tendonitis can attack even a smooth stroker if he happens to accumulate calcium deposits around a shoulder tendon or some other joint. This inflammation often announces itself with such acute pain that the victim can hardly move his arm (or whatever other part is affected). Doctors usually prescribe a local anesthetic or cortisone, plus some sessions with a physical therapist after the inflammation subsides.

You can usually ward off such ailments or minimize their effects if you get regular medical checkups, adjust your game to your physical limitations (see Chapter 18) and equip yourself with whatever adjuncts you may need. For example, Bryan Hamlin, a well-known tournament player in his seventies, always brings along a case which contains the following: absorbent wrist bands, ankle brace, knee brace, elbow brace, antiseptic, moleskin, gauze, scissors, adhesive tape, Band-Aids, cap, eyeshade, thermos of fruit juice, thermos of hot tea, salt tablets, glucose pills, a small towel to tuck in his belt, a large towel, and an extra sweater. Maybe his longevity on the courts is telling us something.

22 / Different Court: Different Game

You'll Be Surprised

With new courts now being built at the rate of five thousand a year, sooner or later you'll probably play on a varied assortment of surfaces. If you learn on one surface, you're in for a jolt the first time you play on some other kind of court.

The game suddenly changes more than you'd believe possible. Your strokes will feel different. The ball will seem to act as no good tennis ball should. The type of game that may have worked beautifully for you, on your accustomed courts, won't work at all on this new one. Even your footwork will play you false: When you run for a ball you'll either get to it too soon or too late. It takes a drastic retuning of all your reactions to adjust your game to a different surface.

Even the great stars frequently fail to make the adjustment—perhaps because their strokes were fine-tuned by hours of practice on one particular surface. Many an international champ on one kind of court has looked futile on another.

Billie Jean King is great on fast cement courts, but Chris Evert has beaten her, 6-0, 6-0, on slow clay. Aussie John Newcombe, winner of national crowns on grass at Wimbledon and Forest Hills, has lost to unseeded players in early rounds of the French and Italian championships that are played on red clay courts.

When the Rumanian stars Ilie Nastase and Ion Tiriac lost all five matches of the Davis Cup finals on Cleveland's cement courts, Nastase told reporters, "We had only ten days to practice on this court. Sure, we beat the British at Wimbledon on grass, but it takes too long to learn how to run on this kind of court." He and Tiriac had learned at home on surfaces that some top internationalists consider the slowest in the world.

A baseline retriever like Cliff Richey was at his best on slow courts. A sledgehammer server like Stan Smith has a big edge when the surface is fast. Arthur Ashe, who learned on dirt courts around Richmond but then enrolled at UCLA and learned all over again on California's cement, may possess two sets of reflexes—and may occasionally get them mixed up, which conceivably could explain his unpredictable streaks of good and mediocre tennis. "The clay instincts are completely different," he says.

If these mighty experts lose their touch when they switch surfaces, how about you? Better watch your step!

What's the Difference?

The chief reason why players have trouble getting used to a different type of court is simply that the ball bounces off the ground at a different speed, and sometimes at a different angle.

A "fast" court is one that makes a ball ricochet like a bullet when it bounces. A "slow" court makes the ball seem to float up after it hits. The fastest of all courts is wood, on which most indoor championships have been played. Next fastest is cement, the original California specialty. Almost as fast is grass, which gave the game its original name of "lawn" tennis, and for generations was the classic setting for the great traditional tournaments of England and the eastern U.S., but is now becoming obsolete because it needs so much maintenance. (At the two dozen old-line eastern clubs that still have grass, members usually can play only four afternoons a week, for three hours at a time. The rest of the week is needed to get the turf back in shape.)

Big corporations like Borden, Chevron, and 3M are competing for the market in all-weather surfacing, which costs from $1,000 to $11,000 per court, and in the newer indoor "carpet" courts of synthetic fabrics or plastics. Naturally the different brands have slightly different speeds. In general I'd say that they rank just below cement for speediness.

Asphalt is slower, and clay or dirt is slowest. Asphalt used to be a common surface for public courts because it was comparatively inexpensive, but it didn't hold up well. When weeds began growing up through the asphalt, players demanded something better. Some contractors have put a layer of plastic over the asphalt, giving it more durability and a faster bounce.

More people play on clay than on any other surface. Some clay courts (especially *en-tout-cas*) dry quickly, which is one of the reasons they're popular in parts of the world that have rain during the summer. Just as the microscopic sponginess of this texture absorbs water, it also cushions the ball. Smash a ball as hard as you please on clay, it will still float up with a high bounce.

Keep Calm on Clay

The big serves are much easier to handle on clay than on fast courts. Even a cannonball smash comes off clay slowly enough so that the average receiver can get a racket on it. Therefore the hard hitters and the net rushers feel frustrated on clay. But the baseline players, the defensive strategists, the retrievers, and the steady ground-strokers who keep getting the ball back—these are the people who enjoy the clay-court matches most.

When you play on clay, the best game is a backcourt game. Don't hit the ball as hard as you would on the faster surfaces; you're just wasting your strength if you do. Try to outsteady your opponent. The steadier player, not the harder hitter, usually wins on clay.

Storming the net isn't as likely to bring you victory on this surface as it is on others. You'll have a tough time putting the ball away. Your overhead smashes will be returned much oftener. Your corner placements will stay in the air so long after they bounce that a good opponent will get to them.

Ease up on your service. Make dead sure that you get the first one in, and forget about power. There's no such thing as a powerful service on clay. By the same token, when you're receiving, step in closer to receive the serve than you would on other courts. That slow bounce will enable you to move up and try for a forcing shot on your return.

If you've been used to playing on faster courts, your strokes will be off. Your timing and coordination will be out of kilter. The reason is that you've been drawing your racket back faster, and swinging it forward faster, in order to hit a fast-bouncing ball. Now, against a slow-bouncing ball, your stroke is speeded up too much and you're hitting the ball too soon. Therefore, try to make yourself slow down. Relax more. Be deliberate. Let your racket float back and forward with a smooth, lazy stroke. Play safe, and wait for the other fellow to make errors.

A clay court must be constantly watered, raked, and brushed. It can't be used in winter because a ball won't bounce on cold ground. Some clubs have indoor clay courts which avoid these disadvantages, but more and more outdoor clubs are switching to cement. We'll consider tactics for cement-court play in a moment. But first let's pause for a few words about grass courts, just in case you're among the upper-income types who sometimes play on them.

Beware of Skids

Grass is tricky. Not only does the ball take a quick bounce, but it skids. Furthermore, the surface is slightly different each time you play because the grass is damper—or drier—than last time.

A good grass court is cropped as close as a putting green, and should have no moisture in it. But a sudden rainstorm can make it so soggy next day that you'll think the ball is bewitched.

On the other hand, when it is in perfect condition, it seems to hold the ball on the ground longer. The ball skids along, then streaks up like a flying fish bouncing over the water. Generally it takes a lower bounce than it will on any other surface.

Therefore you'll want to hit harder, take the net oftener if you have a decent net game, and try to put the ball away. Power pays dividends on grass. Cultivate a sharp serve if you're going to be a grass player. Cultivate your smash at the net.

Switching to grass from clay or asphalt, you'll feel as if you were playing in a deep-sea diving suit. The ball will shoot past you before you even start to hit it. You won't seem to be covering court nearly as fast as usual; actually you're running as fast as you normally do, but the ball isn't waiting for you after it bounces.

So now you've got to speed yourself up. Run faster, and stroke faster. Give yourself a hypo. Get dynamic. Glue your eye on that ball, and start drawing your racket back much earlier than you've been used to. Key yourself up to stroke quickly, without flicking or lunging. However, hang on to your long flowing follow-through or your game *will* go haywire when you try to soup it up. But above all, watch the ball! Remember what we said way back in Chapter 3? You can hit a fast ball—*if* you keep your eye on it.

Back up farther than usual to receive service, if you're having trouble returning it. This is the kind of court where you're in real trouble against a fireball serve. Give yourself the extra time to hit it by taking it farther behind the baseline. The same principle applies if you're trading drives with your opponent. Play deeper than you normally would. The ball won't bounce as high as it does on clay, but it will bounce faster and farther horizontally. The way to handle a low fast bounce is to back up.

Cement Is for Killers

The reason western tennis stars are usually slugging, smashing players is that they're used to cement. The way to win tournaments on cement is to develop the killer instinct. Get a big serve. Get a net game. You can't win from the baseline. So force your way into forecourt—or work your way up, in gentler stages, if the rushing game is too tiring for you—and put the ball away. A hard-hit ball stays hit on this court.

The ball comes off cement just as fast as off grass, and it takes a truer bounce. There's no skid when it hits on a good cement surface. Consequently, it seems to bounce a little higher, although it booms through frighteningly fast. Its bounce is always the same on cement—not low one day and nonexistent another, as you sometimes find on a grass court.

Switching from cement to grass, or the reverse, isn't too hard. Both are fast enough so that you don't have to speed up your reflexes perceptibly. But a change between cement and clay will throw you off badly for a while. Be prepared for the difference in speed, and you'll gradually get geared for it.

Cement courts are becoming more common in all parts of the country, indoors as well as out. They're economical in the long run because they last forever and need very little maintenance. Wash them once a week, and that's it. The court at my home was originally May Sutton Bundy's, put down in 1928. It's still as good as new.

You'd think cement would be harder on the feet than softer surfaces, but it turns out that the opposite is true. Your feet don't slide on cement, so you're far less likely to get blisters. However, the pounding on cement can weaken your arches, so you may want to get tennis shoes with built-in supports fitted to your arches.

If you're thinking of installing a court at your home, or of getting new ones put in at your club, cement is a good buy if you can afford the high initial outlay. Order a green surface, with a dark brown outside the lines for contrast.

But be sure you deal with a contractor who knows exactly what he's doing. Laying down a concrete court is no job for an inexperienced man. Some new eastern courts have been abysmal disappointments because they were put in by contractors who'd never attempted a concrete job before. Since then some experienced western contractors have been journeying east to do excellent jobs. They can even slow the surface down if you prefer, by mixing sand into the top coating of paint to roughen it, although this doesn't make it as slow as clay.

Most synthetic surfaces call for almost the same style of play that you'd use on cement, since they give almost as fast a bounce with no skid. If you're thinking of ordering one, get expert advice, because costs and quality vary widely. The carpet courts (originally developed so barnstorming professionals could roll them up and ship them from place to place for their matches) are popular for indoor installations—but not so popular outdoors, because they don't hold up well under weathering.

Night Court? Drive with Care

Night tennis under lights is becoming popular. But it isn't easy to play, unless the lighting system is one of those new (and extremely costly) ones that are almost as good as daylight.

Under any lights but the very best, you can't see the ball quite as well as you do in sunlight. So it behooves you to be careful. When you're getting set for a drive, watch that ball very closely. The changing light will throw you off if your gaze falters for an instant. You may misjudge its speed, or even its course.

At night, you'll probably find it wise to play the baseline a little more than you do normally. Because of the light, you'll be bothered when you volley. Somehow you don't have time to see the ball soon enough. It's almost down your throat before you realize it's started toward you. Try staying back farther, or playing more of a defense game from back court, and you may get better results.

Whatever the surface or the lighting conditions, think about them before you go on the court. Prepare yourself mentally for the kind of bounce you'll get on that surface. Get yourself consciously slowing down, or speeding up, during the preliminary warm-up. Think about what you're doing, and why you're doing it—and you'll adjust yourself faster to whatever surface you play on.

23 / Tournament Tips

This Means You!

"Who, me? Enter a tournament? Perish forbid. I'd sooner test a new type of parachute," may be approximately your reaction to the thought of signing an entry blank for any tennis tournament whatsoever. But if you'll hold your horses for a moment, and read a little further, maybe I can coax you into perusing this whole chapter, and even into following its advice.

Whoever you are, whatever your grade of tennis, if you take the game seriously enough to read this book then you ought to enter at least one tournament a year. Not because you can win it, necessarily. Not even because you're likely to get beyond the first couple of rounds. But just because it's good medicine. Just because the mere act of playing in a tournament will improve your game and help you to get an edge on your regular playmates in your friendly once-a-week workouts with them.

A tournament—any tournament—sharpens you up. It gives you experience under fire. Win or lose, you come out of it with a little more confidence, a little more savvy, a habit of moving faster and fighting harder.

Maybe you think that you'd be completely outclassed. So, what? Have you anything to lose? Why not take a beating, if necessary, for the sake of the toughening up it will give you? There's nothing disgraceful about going down in love sets in the first round of a tournament. Your friends will respect you for making the attempt. Lots of players enter Forest Hills or Wimbledon in the full knowledge that they'll never win even one game. They get pulverized and go home happy because they acquired what they wanted: experience.

I'm not urging you to sign up for Forest Hills, particularly. A close match in a small tourney will do you more good than a one-sided defeat in a big affair. So what I am urging is that you pick your spot, find the tournament where you'll meet players who are closest to yourself in ability, and enter it even if you think it's too tough for you.

Everybody can lick somebody. You ought to be able to find some division in some tournament where you can at least look as if you know what the score is. If you've never been in competition before, get your first taste of it in the easiest tourney you can find.

There are public parks tournaments. Novice tournaments. Industrial tournaments. Handicap tournaments. Father-and-son events. Veterans' divisions. Junior veterans' divisions. Probably, within fifty miles of where you're sitting at this moment, all kinds of motley mobs are playing in tournaments where anybody who can hit a backhand is considered a star. Find one of these and wade in if you don't feel that you're ready for anything faster.

Anyhow, whatever your ability, let's assume that you're entering some tournament. Maybe it's the club annual tourney, and you've been in it every summer for ten years. Or maybe this is your first event, your baptism of fire. Either way, you'll probably benefit from a few tips.

Before the Battle

You can have a tournament match partly won, or partly lost, before you ever walk onto the court. It depends on how you prepare yourself.

Your preparation can begin a week or more before your first match, if you know who your opponent will be. Maybe you can look him over. If you get the chance, take it. Watch him in action, as long and often as possible. Look for his tender spots. Notice what shots he usually blows. When you play him, you'll want to give him whatever he likes least, so now you ought to be analyzing him from the sidelines. What are his habit patterns? What sort of temperament has he? Read Chapter 3 again and use it in making a study of the man you're to play. Maybe you've known him for years, but you'll still learn things about his game that you never knew before if you'll spend an hour or so systematically studying his actions.

You can carry your scouting a step further, and start mapping your battle plan for your probable second-round opponent too, if the draw is posted early enough. During that week or so before the tournament starts, you'll be smart to watch not only the entry you're scheduled to play first, but the two other players who'll be battling for the second-round bracket against you, if they seem to be about even bets. Do as much advance planning as you can. You'll be amazed to find what a difference it makes when you're in there playing the actual matches. It's a cinch your opponents won't have any particular strategy figured out, except simply to play their normal game, so if you can make them play in a style to which they're not accustomed, they're likely to start coming apart at the seams.

Practice will help you too, in the week before the tourney starts. Not just ordinary practice, with your usual buddies. But practice with someone whose game is as similar as possible to the man you're going up against. If you'll be playing a net rusher, work out with the best volleyer you can coax onto the court with you. If your man hugs the baseline, forget about the forecourt boys and find somebody who'll keep feeding you long drives from far back.

If you can't get the kind of sparring partner you want, at least try to simulate battle conditions with whomever you do get. In your tournament match, are you planning to hammer the other fellow's backhand, or his forehand? Are you going to try to lob him to death, or volley him off the court, or outsteady him from the baseline? Whatever you're planning, practice it relentlessly in advance. Maybe it's not the way to beat the fellow you're practicing with. Do it anyway. Get used to it—so used to it that you'll do it without thinking when the pace gets hot.

Need I say that a good night's sleep, on the eve of a tournament match, always helps? Pass up the coffee and cognac and cigars for that one night, at least. Steer clear of the bright lights. Go to bed early. You'll have a much happier time on the court next day.

On the day of the match, eat a good meal—but not too good—about two or three hours before you're due to play. Trained athletes usually take some soup, meat, and vegetables, and a light dessert. They generally pass up milk and coffee, in favor of tea or water. It's only the hamfats and knotheads who rush off to fortify themselves with a hamburger and milk shake just before going on the court, or take a stiff guzzle of firewater to "steady their nerves." If you happen to draw that kind of opponent, congratulations! You'll have him feeling as though he's playing in a diving suit if you can just make him run for a set or two. Pull him up with chop strokes and drop shots, then chase him back with lobs, and he'll soon start dragging his feet.

It's Nice to Be Nervous

Nearly all the best players are nervous wrecks before a match. They sleep as if they'd made their bed on a nest of fire ants. For hours on the day of the match, their stomach feels as if they'd swallowed an alarm clock. They totter onto the court like a prisoner being led before a firing squad. Even after years of competition, they still get the meemies before every big battle. But they don't mind because they know it's Nature's way of tightening them up for a supreme effort. They also know that they'll feel much better once the match has actually started.

So you shouldn't mind, either, if you're nervous. You should be glad. It's a symptom of real competitive fire inside you. The only time you need worry about pregame nervousness is when you don't feel any. If you're calm and unworried before a match, then, brother, look out! Old Man Overconfidence hath you in thrall, and you're likely to be eaten alive by any opponent who really wants to win.

So welcome that wobbly feeling. It means you'll be keyed up, with plenty of adrenaline surging into your system. About a half hour before your match, you should begin working off some of the nervousness by rallying with someone on a vacant court. Stroke the ball back and forth for ten or fifteen minutes. Take practice serves. Move to the net and volley a bit. Finish off with a couple of good lively exchanges where you do a little hard running and jumping, to make sure your legs are well warmed up. This whole session shouldn't last more than a quarter hour, and during that quarter hour there's one thing you should be thinking about, above all else. That is to relax.

Keep dinning that thought into your head during the warm-up. Be loose as ashes. Make your strokes graceful and flowing. Take it easy. Feel the ball. Forget about hitting hard, and hit smoothly. Relax. . . . Relax. . . . Relax. . . . Be smooth. . . . Be smooth. . . . Be smooth. If you keep thinking about this while you're getting ready, you'll be more likely to do it when the match starts, and it will help you immensely.

Look Sharp

At last it's time for your match, and you're called onto the court. The way you walk out, and the way you act during the preliminary rallying with your opponent, are important. Much more important than most club players realize.

As you come on the court, you should look happy, eager, full of pep. Don't hurry, but be on your toes. Be sharp. Be smiling. Your eyes should be snapping, your face beaming with the sheer joy of being alive.

Talk to your opponent, briskly and happily. Say something like, "Isn't this a perfect day for tennis? Nice and bright. I love this hot weather." The hotter the day, the more you should pretend to like it. Or if it's dark and gloomy, you should enthuse about the cool bracing air. No matter what the weather, it should be "wonderful for tennis" in your opinion.

The same goes for whatever else you mention to your opponent. Everything is dandy. God's in His Heaven; all's right with the world. You're delighted that So-and-So is to be umpire; he's tops. You're glad the match is to be played on this particular court; you were hoping it would be.

There's something oddly discouraging to your opponent in seeing you so happy. He's secretly feeling as if he were starting over Niagara in a barrel, and it doesn't help his state of mind to watch you bouncing around the court with such horrible heartiness. The thought that he feels terrible and you don't is sometimes enough to give him a bad inferiority complex before he even hits the first ball.

Watch your man closely while you're warming up with him. If you haven't seen him play before, you'll need this time to size up his strokes and spot a weakness or two, or learn to anticipate some of his shots. If you know his game, you still should be studying him to see if he's off form today. Maybe he's hitting the ball too hard through nervousness. Or maybe he's got "steel elbow"—a malady that often attacks inexperienced players in a tournament match. It means poking at the ball with an inflexibly bent elbow instead of smoothly stroking through it. Many players who have beautiful flowing strokes in practice suddenly stiffen up in a match. Watch for signs of this.

If you find anything wrong with your opponent's game, swarm all over it the minute the match starts. If he has steel elbow, storm the net. He can't possibly pass you while he's poking the ball. If he's hitting too hard, stay back and just keep returning the ball. He'll make the errors. If his serve is off, move up close to receive it. If his overhead isn't working, lob him crazy. Get the jump on him somehow, in the first few games, and you may run him right off the court.

Win Your War of Nerves

A tournament tennis match is a war of nerves. If a player's nerves get jangled, he loses some of his coordination and misses the precision shots that pay off. So it's up to you to keep yourself on an even keel psychologically—and to do whatever you can, ethically, to disturb and discourage the other fellow.

You'll bother him no end if you look completely unruffled when you miss an easy shot or when a close decision is called against you. He expects you to be annoyed. If you're not, he'll wonder why. He'll decide that you must be so certain of winning that a point or two makes no difference to you. This will worry him. Or it may make him mad. Either way, you've shaken him up psychologically, and he won't play quite as well.

You'll also wear him down mentally if you keep up that brisk, happy front you wore when you walked onto the court. Stay on your toes. Look alive. Make believe you're enjoying the game immensely. When you make a good shot, comment jovially on it. Say something like, "Boy, the luck is sure running my way today!" or "This must be my day." Such gentle reminders that things are going well for you will be strictly bad for your opponent's peace of mind. And somehow, by an odd sort of self-hypnosis, they're good for your own mental outlook.

Even when you get tired, pretend that you're not. Bill Tilden won at least one of his toughest matches by that simple deception. In 1926, in his championship battle with Jean Borotra, he trailed two sets to one after three demoniac sets in the broiling sun. But as Borotra staggered away to the dressing room for the rest period, Tilden sat down nonchalantly at the court side, and waited impatiently there until the fagged Frenchman returned. There was more zing than ever in Tilden's first few strokes. Borotra fell apart, and Tilden ran out the match. He revealed afterward that he'd been at the point of collapse himself.

Nervousness, in one form or another, has wrecked many fine players in big matches. The late Perry Jones, the brains of the southern California tennis machine, gave his tournament stars a nine-word formula for victory:

"Watch the ball, hit it hard, and don't think."

This is a blunt way of phrasing some subtle tennis wisdom. It points out three ailments that are likely to afflict anybody during a tight match: taking eyes off the ball, pushing it instead of stroking it, and worrying about form.

Even Stan Smith forgets to watch the ball sometimes, in the heat of battle. It costs him points. Everybody else, good or bad, lets his eye stray—the good players only now and then, the bad ones constantly. I've mentioned this matter before, but there's no harm in harping on it again: you must keep reminding yourself, over and over, to glue your eye on the ball while you're serving, stroking, or waiting for it to come to you.

As for the second point of the Jones formula: in a match, there's a tendency to get scared, and consequently to poke the ball instead of hitting freely. Fear of making errors leads to choking up. Many a topnotch player has shoved the ball like a schoolgirl when the pressure of a big match tightened him up. Don't let it get you. Keep loose. Hit the ball, don't push it!

When Perry Jones said "Don't think!" he doesn't mean that you should forget strategy, anticipation, or attempts to outwit the other fellow. He means you shouldn't think about how you're hitting the ball as you hit it. Just do what comes naturally while you stroke. Never try to analyze your form in the middle of a match. It's downright disastrous.

I made this discovery during my college days at the University of California at Berkeley. I played a match with Dan Robertson when I was sick and would have been in bed if I'd had any sense. The match figured to be about 6—1, 6—1 in Dan's favor. But Dan and I were good friends who liked to chat with each other a bit as we played, and I happened to remark early in the match that his forehand looked strange. Instead of trouncing me, he lost 6—1, 6—2. He was thinking about his forehand.

This was dirty tennis, of course, and I wouldn't have used it intentionally. Don't let anybody use it on you. Whatever betide, don't think about how you're stroking while the match is in progress.

Don't drink too much water, either, during a hot and thirsty match. The water cup has been the downfall of many an inexperienced tournament entry. Just sip a little, to rinse your mouth and throat, then spit it out. Do this every time you change courts, if you feel dry, but don't swallow more than a mouthful or two. It won't kill you to feel thirsty until the match is over. In fact, it will be better for you than slaking your thirst. A glass or two of water can slow you down to a stumble in a strenuous tennis set. It can give you dull pains in the midsection, or even nausea. So lay off.

Watch your temper, too. When you're keyed up and fighting hard to win, there'll be great provocation to explode at a bum decision by the umpire or a boggled shot by yourself. Don't give in to that frothing and fermenting inside your skull. Nobody ever made a friend for himself by shouting or scowling on a tennis court. Any display of temper not only encourages your foe but dismays your friends. It's bad manners, bad sportsmanship, and bad character. You don't feel any better afterward, and your opponent's game picks up because he thinks you're going to pieces. So you lose from every angle if you give in to temper.

Some players whine and complain when a match is running against them. This is stupid strategy too. Any sign of being discouraged or downhearted gives a psychological lift to their opponent. Keep smiling, even if you're spraying your shots over all the fences. And keep fighting. Even if you're playing a champ, there's hope until the last set is over. Many a star has gotten overconfident and blown a match that was in the bag for him. The best player in the world can flub shots, can hit wild streaks, can throw away a two-set lead. So if you get behind, keep calm and figure how to change your game. Think over Chapters 8 and 9 and try some of the techniques in them. Play the match out to the end with the best that's in you, and you'll feel good about it afterward—win or lose.

24 / How to Buy Equipment

Don't Overspend

Most tennis enthusiasts spend far more on equipment than they need to. They're equipment crazy. They're forever trying new rackets, new stringing, different makes of shoes or balls. They're like hypochondriacs who keep buying new pills and medicines they don't need. The cure lies in hard work and common sense, not in buying a lot of gimmicks.

Actually, the costliest equipment is not the best for club players. This is especially true of stringing. Don't have your racket strung with the best gut. Use a less expensive gut, or even nylon. You'll make just as good shots with it unless you're a tournament fiend who plays daily all year round and has developed razor-sharp accuracy. A really topnotch player loses a little of his sharpness without the best gut stringing—a few of his shots go just out when they would have been just in if he'd had the best—but a club player can never tell any difference. His touch isn't that keen to begin with.

Furthermore, nylon gives an infrequent player better service. Dampness hurts gut. Anyone who uses gut stringing has to have his racket restrung every month or so; otherwise the gut deteriorates into something worse than nylon.

It's easy to overspend on rackets, too. Every tennis shop has customers who keep coming back to try out different rackets. Such addicts buy several new ones, all different, in the course of a single season. What do they gain by it? Nothing. Actually, they weaken their game.

Youngsters should start with a ten- or twelve-dollar lightweight wood racket. Aluminum rackets are too expensive for beginners. Adults should beg or borrow various rackets in their first few weeks of play, experimenting until they find one that feels comfortable. They'll probably stay with it for years.

Imagination can enter into our preferences for rackets. I remember that Bobby Riggs, who carried six identical rackets in his championship days, became convinced one day that a certain racket was better than the other five. It had just exactly the feel and balance he wanted. Some infinitesimal difference in its manufacture gave it a little extra something that made a big difference in his game, he felt. So he made up his mind to use that racket henceforth, and to try to have the manufacturer duplicate it. All well and good—except that the next day, when he tried to pick out that racket from among the six, he couldn't tell which one it was!

Another famous pro once ordered a set of rackets made to his usual specifications. When they arrived, he was furious. They all felt too heavy. So he handed them back to the manufacturer's representative, who apologized profusely and brought back another set a week later. "Now, these are perfect," the pro exulted. "Just exactly the way I like them. Why couldn't your company make them this way last time?" The representative said something soothing, and departed. He knew better than to let the pro learn that these were the same rackets, unchanged, which had felt "much too heavy" the week before.

What's Your Racket?

Before settling down to one style of racket for yourself, however, you'd better make sure it's the right kind for you. Many once-a-week players handicap themselves needlessly by using a racket that's definitely wrong for them.

A common mistake is buying one that's too light. A light racket feels easy to swing, and thereby fools many people. They don't realize that it won't give them enough wallop. I'd say that any person of normal size and strength should use at least a 13-7/8-ounce racket. The 13-ounce racket, which many buy, is really designed for women with their smaller hands and less muscular arms. Even such a small man as Ken Rosewall, depending on delicate touch rather than slugging, uses a 14-ounce racket.

A few lean to the other extreme and try to swing such a heavy club that it slows them up and tires them out. Unless you're in tiptop condition and play a lot of tennis, or are built like Paul Bunyan, you're better not to buy anything much heavier then a 14-3/4. The chances are that you'll find a 14-1/4 feels better. Great internationalists have been known to use a 15 or even 15-1/2-ounce racket, but I don't recommend such weights for club players.

There is a gadget called the Jamar grip testing device that measures forearm gripping power. The average international tournament player has a gripping power of approximately 105 pounds. The average adult male club player registers about an 80-pound grip, and the average adult female has a gripping power of about 50 pounds. The circumference of forearm muscle mass follows the same pattern: tournament player 11-3/4 inches, average male player 11-1/8 inches, average female player 9-3/8 inches.

This pattern shows you why tournament players can use heavier rackets than the average club man, and why women who don't play constantly are more comfortable with still lighter rackets than their masculine counterparts. All good tennis shops have sensitive scales, and you should weigh your racket before buying it, with the foregoing suggested weights in mind. You can't tell much from the *L, M,* or *H* on the racket handle. They mean light, medium, or heavy, but they're only approximations. There is no recognized standard. One manufacturer's *L* racket may be another's *M.* In general *L* corresponds to less than 13-1/2 ounces strung weight, *M* between 13-1/2 and 14 ounces strung weight, and *H* over 14 ounces. This delicate matter of fractions of an ounce suggests a reason why you'll do better buying your racket from a good sporting goods store or tennis shop, and listening to the advice you get there. Department stores and resort hotels may not know as much about rackets, and probably don't have a good pair of scales handy.

Occasionally someone buys a racket that's heavy in the head or in the handle. A few stars prefer them one way or the other—believing that a head-heavy racket gives a harder serve, or a head-light one is quicker on the volley. But most experts will tell you that the racket should be perfectly balanced; head-heavy ones will swing through too fast, and head-light ones lag behind the wrist. You can experiment for yourself, but at least in the beginning you'll almost certainly find that a balanced racket suits you best. Test yours by putting your finger under the racket at its throat, where the handle joins the head. If it balances evenly from that position, it's okay for weight distribution.

Rackets usually are available with four sizes of handle. The handles come in various shapes ranging from almost round to almost square. Try them all, and decide which grip fits your own hand best. Naturally a big man should have a big grip, and vice versa. Most adult male hands correlate nicely with the standard available sizes of 4-1/2 to 4-3/4 inches, but the average measurement in female hands (from thumb crease to radial border of the ring finger) is 4-1/8 inches, while racket handles of that circumference are hard to buy without a special order. This is why many women play with racket handles that are a bit too big for them.

The shape of the handle is a matter of individual taste, although if I were you I'd be cautious about picking anything on the roundish side. I have trouble feeling just where my grip is if the corners of the handle aren't fairly well defined.

As for stringing, I can't give you a definite figure because no two machines show the same figure for the same pressure. Sixty pounds pressure on my stringing machine may be seventy pounds on someone else's. All I can say is that your racket shouldn't be strung so tight that it's like a board, nor so loosely that you can push the stringing inward perceptibly when you press your hand against it. Try bouncing the racket face against your hand. If you get a high *peeng* and can feel the handle vibrate, then your racket is too taut. If you get a dull *plud* it's too loose. Any good tennis shop can help you tell the difference. Beginners should use rackets a little less tight than normal, so the gut won't wear out as fast; the difference in strokes doesn't become important until a player has had considerable experience.

If you play for blood, and don't mind the cost, you can tell the shop to string your racket a little tighter than usual. It will play better but the string job won't last as long.

Wood, Steel, or Aluminum?

In recent years there has been excitement about the steel tennis racket introduced by René Lacoste, the old-time French star, and about the aluminum rackets sold by several manufacturers. Since 1970 players have been able to choose between three materials for their rackets, and have debated the choice endlessly.

The steel racket is made of chrome-plated tubing and stainless wire, a frame supposedly more durable and resilient than wood, much like the steel-shafted golf clubs which first gave Lacoste the idea. It has an open throat that reduces its wind resistance. The theory is that this lets a player hit faster and harder shots with less effort.

The aluminum racket is the outgrowth of new technology in the aerospace industry, which developed the alloys and extrusion processes to make a good tennis racket. Usually it is a bit shorter than a wood model, and round instead of oval. It has an open throat like the steel one. If the makers' claims for durability come true, the maximum potential sales are one racket to every player in the world.

Both kinds of racket take conventional nylon or gut stringing, just as wooden rackets do. Some tournament stars have tried steel and are enthused; some have done likewise with aluminum.

Metal rackets come in all degrees of whippiness, even more springy than the most flexible wood. Big servers often like this flexibility, and some say that the ball comes off their steel racket so fast that opponents can't tell where it's going. Clark Graebner, one of the early enthusiasts for steel, said, "I like the feel of the ball on the strings. For me, it's easier to serve and volley. It gives you more touch and you can make more flick shots."

However, most players have their doubts. They can't seem to control the ball as well. "It seems that you just tip the ball and it goes over the baseline," one told me. "It takes a lot of getting used to. I've found it good for certain shots and not so good for others."

Dennis Ralston says the aluminum racket is easier to get used to than steel because it's less resilient and the ball doesn't spring off the surface as hard. Aluminum definitely is lighter, and therefore easier for the average woman to handle. I use an aluminum racket all day in giving lessons because it's less tiring—but I'd still rather play a wood racket because I get better feel with it.

I think the difference in the three rackets (ignoring cost for the moment) is mostly a matter of feel. Very early in this book—in Chapter 2—I explained that "feeling" the ball, meeting it squarely and solidly and following through so it feels good against your racket, is the big secret of ball control. Many of today's top men players used steel or aluminum for a season or two then went back to wood because they decided they'd lost some of their feel. In other words, their timing wasn't quite as good. Maybe this is a matter of which racket you use in your formative years.

The steel rackets came on the market at about $10 to $20 more than first-class wooden rackets cost, and so did the aluminum ones, which carried a five-year guarantee later reduced to one year. Maybe the longer life of a metal racket will equalize the price differential. At any rate, I'd advise you to do some experimenting with borrowed rackets before you invest in a high-quality racket of any material. And let their "feel" be your guide.

Take Care!

Treat your racket right if you want to get good service from it. Keep a cover on it; damp air is the natural enemy of tennis rackets. When you have it shellacked, make sure that pure white shellac is used, with only a little thinner.

Picking up balls with your tennis racket is a sure way to wear the racket out faster. Every time you scrape the top of your racket across the ground, in order to get a stationary ball moving and scoop it up, you rub a little of the wood off your racket's rim. Do it long enough, and you'll break the strings where they are laced through the edge. If you can't break yourself of the habit of picking up balls this way, or if you're too creaky jointed to bend down for them, at least you ought to cover the top of your racket with adhesive tape so it won't get worn out so fast.

Your shoes ought to be good quality—either white leather or white canvas-and-rubber. The leather ones are more fashionable, more comfortable, and give more support. Therefore they are also more expensive.

Whatever kind you buy, don't wear them too long, because the soles get dangerously smooth after a while. Make sure there's a good substantial cushion in the sole. They shouldn't fit too tightly because you need to stop suddenly and change direction fast on a tennis court. Therefore you want a little "give" in your shoes; otherwise you'll get footsore. Of course your socks should supply most of this give. Heavy white sweat socks are a must. Get shoes that fit fairly snugly over these but still let you wiggle your toes. If your feet tend to feel too hot when you play tennis, or if they blister easily, try wearing another pair of very light socks underneath the sweat socks. They'll minimize friction and keep your feet cooler because of the layer of air between the two thicknesses of fabric.

New Balls

You should buy new balls every time you play. That's the only way to get a dependable bounce. The difference between a fresh ball and a day-old ball affects the timing of even an ordinary player. The experts can't get along with the same balls for as much as a single afternoon. Even when they're playing informally, just for fun, they open a can of new balls every set. And in tournaments, of course, the balls are usually changed every ninth game.

Buy standard quality balls—one of the well-known brands. And buy them where you know the seller will replace a ball that proves to be dead when it comes out of the can. This happens fairly often, particularly at a big store which buys a whole warehouseful of balls at one time. A ball will lose its freshness sometimes even in an airtight can. The longer a can lies on a shelf before it's opened, the more chance that one or several of its balls will be dead. A good dealer will stand behind every ball he sells. If one has no bounce, he'll give you another one, or even a whole new can of them. Even in a shop that has a fast turnover, a bum ball crops up occasionally. That's why all smart tennis players buy from a dealer with a solid reputation.

Tennis needn't be a rich man's game. A top-grade racket at secondhand, with gut stringing, is within the reach of almost everyone. If well cared for, it will last a long time. White tennis clothes and good shoes can fit into a modest budget. The only item on which you can't stint at all is on balls—and if you make the balls the stake in your game, and follow the tennis techniques outlined in this book, how can you lose?

25 / The Unwritten Laws

Etiquette Is Important

Tennis is more than a way to work up a sweat. It's also a form of sociable good time. It's a way of getting together with your friends for mutual fun—just as a dinner party is, or a dance, or a bridge game. At any social gathering, there are certain unwritten rules of polite behavior. Tennis is no exception. It has its own etiquette.

Etiquette is a stuffy-sounding word. But the underlying meaning of etiquette is simply consideration for other people. When acquaintances gather around a tennis court, they are as considerate of each other (and of nearby strangers) as they would be in a restaurant or on a fishing trip. Tennis etiquette is a set of procedures to help everyone enjoy the game to the utmost.

Manners begin with what you wear—the indication of your respect for the sport and its surroundings. Traditional garb is white, from top to toe, although soft blue and yellow are now well accepted, and even the brighter colors won't stamp you as a lowbrow unless you're in a conservative club.

Men usually wear a knit shirt, always short-sleeved. You'll want the kind with extra-length shirttail in back to keep it from pulling out when you stretch for a high shot. A sleeveless undershirt won't do, even on public courts or backyard courts. Playing stripped to the waist looks crude.

Either shorts or slacks are right, but shorts should be the tailored tennis kind or the knee-length variety known as Bermuda or walking shorts. You'll embarrass your friends if you show up in a pair of short and shiny basketball shorts, or in swim trunks.

The Sin of Snobbery

Does all this talk about correct clothes sound snobbish? It isn't, really. White clothes are no more expensive than colored clothes. There's nothing snobbish about expecting people to know how to dress. It's just a convention, like knowing how to send an invitation and how to set silverware on a table. It makes the occasion a little smoother and pleasanter for everybody involved.

Unfortunately, however, there is some snobbery around tennis clubs. A snob is definitely no gentleman—and no sportsman. The unwritten code among real tennis people frowns severely on hurting anyone's feelings. It goes back to the famous definition of a gentleman by that true Southern aristocrat, General Robert E. Lee, who wrote: "A gentleman is a man who never makes anyone feel inferior."

We all know the tennis snob who tilts his nose at anyone who can't play quite as well as he. This is the tennis variety of social climber. He—or she, more frequently—is always trying to inveigle much better players into games. Good for prestige, you know, to be seen on the court with the better players. Such people will intrigue and push and contrive, making downright nuisances of themselves in their campaign to get a game with superior players. But what a deep freeze they give to any inferior player—even slightly inferior—who ventures to ask them for a game!

These climbers might as well carry large signs lettered "I Am a Snob." They've labeled themselves that plainly. Yet they always seem puzzled because the polite society of tennis is cool to them. That's the way of the pushers and climbers in any group, I suppose. They never quite belong, and they never understand why.

In tennis, a real sportsman and gentleman takes pains to invite weaker players into a game occasionally. And he never asks stronger players for a game. He waits for the invitation to come from them.

Obviously it's more fun to play someone as good as or better than yourself. But if you're well brought up, you don't think only of yourself. You try to give pleasure to your acquaintances sometimes, even if it means sacrificing a little of your own pleasure. So you take on an inferior player now and then, purely as a courtesy to him.

As for superior players, you realize that you may embarrass them by asking for a game. They prefer to practice with people of their own ability, just as you do. Why confront them with the awkward alternative of refusing or playing a game they don't want to play? When they feel in a noble mood, maybe they'll offer to take you on. So you wait until they do. You'd lose caste in their eyes if you asked them. It would be almost the social equivalent of asking them to give you a little money, or asking them to let you move into their home for a few days.

You're Weighed by Your Words

What a player says, and how he says it, makes a big difference to his standing among well-bred tennis people.

The wrong words, or even the wrong tone of voice, can stigmatize a player. This works the other way too. A player can win himself some quiet admiration by saying the right thing at the right time.

For example, a player should seem to be enjoying the game even when he isn't. He should compliment the other players on their good shots. How often have you won a point with a sizzling play, and walked back in a pleasant glow of satisfaction, only to see your opponent scowling and cursing himself, maybe even grumbling "I sure gave you a set-up that time, didn't I?" or "Gosh, I'm terrible today." It spoils all all your fun. Only a boor makes such remarks.

The unwritten tennis code demands that a player compliment his opponent for winning, console him for losing. A sportsman says "You were terrific today" when he loses, not "I couldn't do a thing right." He says "I played over my head" when he wins, not "I was only fair today."

When a player is asked to play with someone weaker, if he doesn't feel generous and self-sacrificing at the moment there's no reason why he should accept. But he is obliged, if he's a gentleman, to refuse gently. He can say something like, "Right now I'm waiting for someone else, but if he doesn't get here I'd love to play you later today," or "Thanks a lot for the invitation. Can't tackle you right now because I'm trying to find a fellow I'm supposed to play. But I'll hunt you up later, if I can, and we'll have a set."

The cold, distant refusal, the transparent evasion of "I'll let you know later," or the blunt "It wouldn't be any fun" are always bad manners. They're snobbish. They make the other fellow feel inferior. Of course, he was guilty of an error in the first place in asking for a game, if he's not as strong a player as the man he asked. But that doesn't make it permissible to snub him. Snubbing just isn't permissible, ever, by people who believe in good manners.

Nor is it permissible to stand somebody up. An engagement is inviolate among sportsmen. If a man can't keep a date to play tennis, he is supposed to telephone and let the other fellow know, well ahead of time. If he's going to be late, he sends word. Only a serious difficulty keeps him from being present, on the dot, for any date—tennis or otherwise.

Yet I've seen a few supposedly well-bred members of tennis clubs blandly break dates because someone better happened along and was willing to play them. When the original opponent showed up, he was told, "Terribly sorry, I forgot all about having promised to play Joe here," so he was left with nobody to play. It's a cheap trick and nobody with innate decency ever stoops to it. Regardless of how keenly he wants to play someone else, the tennis square-shooter sticks to his original engagement.

Another sign of a real aristocrat in a tennis club is that he's sociable with newcomers. If he sees a stranger sitting in lonely solitude on the sidelines, obviously wanting to play but afraid to ask anyone, he'll at least strike up a conversation and probably get the new arrival into a game. Cliques and clannishness don't go with good manners.

Gambling doesn't go, either. That's hard for some players to realize. They can't seem to get fun out of tennis unless they play for ten dollars or more a set. And yet they wonder why they have such a small circle of friends at the tennis club!

Asking to play for money is a sure way to repel the better elements in tennis. Playing for the drinks, or the balls, isn't considered gambling, and it's all right with nearly everyone. But $10 a set definitely is considered gambling, and is frowned on. I know plenty of wealthy men around our tennis club who could lose $100 a set and never feel it. But they politely decline to play for anything more than the cost of the drinks. They know that betting leads to hard feelings, that it's a dangerous example for youngsters around the courts, that it takes tennis out of the realm of amateur sport and puts it into a smelly unhealthy atmosphere of furtive professionalism. Any club that lets gambling flourish develops into a hangout for tennis sharks who hunt for "pigeons"—for suckers, in other words, who can be conned into playing for big stakes by being allowed to win a few times at smaller stakes. I've seen more than one innocent lose his entire savings on a tennis court. Real sportsmen don't mix tennis and gambling.

Quiet, Please!

Another rule of tennis etiquette forbids loud noises. A player who is concentrating on his serve can be thrown out of kilter by someone yelling across the courts, "What's the score?" or "What time is it?" or "Phone call for So-and-So!" Among courteous players, and spectators too, a quiet voice is the right voice. If a call comes to the club for someone who's on the courts, the message is relayed to him privately instead of across an acre of intervening tennis players. When a spectator wants to know how a match is going, he walks to the court and asks one of the players quietly, during a lull, instead of screeching at him from the veranda.

The rule goes double for swearing. A stream of loud oaths from a tennis player simply marks him as coarse and unintelligent.

A polished player, whether on a public court or a private one, never does anything that disturbs other players. He never shows anger, never betrays boredom, never gets obnoxious in any way. If one of his balls rolls onto a neighboring court, he waits until play has paused on that court before asking for the ball. If there are players waiting and no vacant courts, he speeds up play a little, doesn't stoop to fudging about the score, and gives up the court as soon as the set is over. Quixotic? I don't think so. He wants other players to do the same for him, and he knows that courtesy is contagious. A few good examples soon shame other people into following them.

Need I add that the unwritten laws of tennis also require a player to give his opponent the benefit of the doubt on a close line shot? Anything else would be cheating. If he really has no idea whether a ball landed in or out, and no one else saw it, he suggests playing the point over. That's nothing more than common honesty.

The tennis code, after all, crystallizes into the Golden Rule. Just be considerate of everyone else, treat them as you'd like to be treated, and you'll never go wrong.

26 / So You're on the Tournament Committee

Must Club Tourneys Be Dull?

The average tournament in the average club is greeted with deafening apathy by most members. After all, why should they whoop and holler and send up skyrockets for it? They know pretty well who the semifinalists will be, and probably even who the champ will be. Anybody else who enters is simply in there as cannon fodder. So most of the members stay away.

It's the same sad story in playground tournaments, school tournaments, and minor public-park tournaments. Small participation. No gallery. Not much fun for anybody.

Must it be ever thus? Can't a tournament committee do anything to get mobs of people playing or watching?

The answers are respectively no and yes, for my dollar.

A club tourney—or a tourney in any other organized group—needn't be dull. It can attract players of all ages, sizes, shapes, and abilities. It can draw a big gallery of excited onlookers. All that's needed is a tournament committee to do a little imaginative planning.

If you're on the tournament committee, shake it up a bit. Throw in some new ideas. Look for novelty. Plan to hold a tournament every month or so—a different kind each time.

Mix 'em Up

The way to get everybody talking about a tournament, and playing in it, is to make it new and different. Rig it so that everybody has a chance, and nobody knows who'll come out on top.

Here's what I mean. Run a doubles tournament with the strongest players teamed up with the weakest, to make all the tandems as nearly equal in strength as the tournament committee can figure. Another time run a family doubles tournament: father-and-son teams, or husband-and-wife, or maybe just any two members of a family paired together.

Get up a Class B tournament some month, strictly for the mediocre players. You'll probably attract more entries than you ever did for the "big" club tournament open to all members.

Another month try a round-robin tournament. Here's how it works, in case you've never seen one. Divide the players into groups of six. Then each sixsome has its own private little tournament. Every player in it plays every other player, so he has five matches in all. But each match lasts only six games. A player rotates against each other player in his group, playing six games with each. Then whichever player has won the highest total of games—thirty games would be the maximum possible, of course—is the winner in his own little round robin. The winners in each group of six then play off for the championship, probably in regulation two-out-of-three-set matches.

The feature that puts firecrackers in a round robin is dividing up the sixsomes according to ability so that all six players bracketed together are about the same strength. Then they really get steamed up about the tourney. They're getting a chance to go up against five different opponents of their own class—something that may not have happened to them for years. You know how it is in the average tennis club. Each member has a few cronies and plays with them all the time, never meeting anybody else. Just breaking up those tight little circles temporarily, throwing everybody in contact with different players, is enough to make this kind of a tourney a big success. It often leads to lots of new friendships and a wider circle of sparring partners for everybody who signs up.

This type of tournament can be run off in one weekend, or even in a single afternoon, if the tournament committee stays on top of it to keep the players rotating quickly, without confusion. Nobody minds too much if the winners of the sixsomes aren't well matched. They've had their fun already. The play-offs are pretty much of a formality, to satisfy the victory-minded aces who insist on a fight to the finish.

Another way to make a big splash some dull·afternoon is to get up a costume tournament, in which the players have to play in full regalia, and prizes are given for the best costumes, with only minor prizes for the best playing. It's comedy stuff, strictly for laughs, but everybody loves it. Here at our own club I've seen men play in Mexican blankets and sombreros, or hauling a full set of golf clubs around the court with them. You could hear the laughing for blocks.

If you want a tournament to boom along more or less indefinitely, get a ladder tourney started. Stack the club membership up according to ability, with the best men at the top, and allow a player to challenge anyone who is five rungs or less above him. If the lower player wins, the two change places on the ladder.

How to Handicap

The biggest and hottest tourney, the one that keeps stars and weaklings and all kinds of in-betweeners on their toes, the one that pulls spectators like a dogfight is a handicap tournament. That is, provided the handicapping is done right.

Too many tournament committees pull the boner of handicapping by games. That is, they'll say to Joe Champ, "You're to be handicapped three games in every set." They give other players varying handicaps—minus two games, or plus one, or whatever they think is right.

This doesn't work. It's no good. The strong players still win all their matches, the duffers don't get beyond the first or second round. Why? Because a good player can whip a weak one 6–2 or even 6–0 when he turns on the heat. It happens constantly, even among big-league tournament players. So the run-of-the-club players aren't helped at all by starting a set with a lead of several games. A stronger opponent will still walk away with the set every time.

The way to handicap is by points, not by games.

Give the poorest player in the club a plus-40 start in every game he plays. Plaster a minus-40 handicap on the classiest player. Everybody in between gets whichever of the five intermediate scores seems to suit his strength: a minus-30 or minus-15 for the better players, a love or plus-15 or plus-30 for the weaker ones. ˙

This really gives everyone a fighting chance against anyone else. Suppose the club ace and the club dub happen to meet. The ace is 40 points in the hole at the beginning of each game, and the dub is 40 points to the good. The ace has to win three points in a row just to bring the score to love—40, and three more to make it deuce. If the dub snatches just one point among the first six, he wins the game! This kind of handicap really makes the stars walk a tightrope. A single slip, and they've dropped a game. As often as not, some downtrodden and despised weakling arises and knocks the champ out of the running. No wonder the lesser players get excited about a handicap tourney, and the crowd gathers round to watch the club's Mr. Unbeatable fighting for his life.

When players of intermediate strength tangle with each other, the scorekeeping will be simplified if handicaps are cancelled out as much as possible. That is, if a plus-15 player meets a plus-30 player, simply call the score 15—love at the beginning of each game. If a minus-15 meets a plus-15, start the game at 30—love.

One word of caution. In deciding how much to handicap each player, you'll be smart not to trust to the judgment of the tournament committee. Get a group of players together, representing a cross section of all levels of strength, and let them work out the handicaps. If the handicapping balances everyone pretty evenly, then you'll come up with a tournament that the whole club will talk about for months afterward.

Stage It with Showmanship

Whatever kind of tournament you select, be sure to run it with verve and color. Make a big thing of the finals. Have the trophies all in glittering array on a table beside the court. Get a properly dressed referee and a couple of linesmen. Build up the finals with as much publicity as you can: word-of-mouth publicity, posters on the bulletin boards, even an item or two in the sport pages of the local newspapers. Have a clever master of ceremonies on hand to present the trophies immediately after the match.

And be sure to arrange for a gala party in the clubhouse, ready to get rolling as soon as the trophies are awarded.

Don't feel that you need something huge and silver-plated for your trophies. These special handicap tourneys and novelty tourneys and the like are just as successful if the trophies are small, just as long as they look well on somebody's mantel. A beer mug, to be imprinted with the winner's name, makes a highly satisfactory trophy. So does a champagne glass, or a Moscow Mule Cup, if it's prettied up with several yards of ribbon and properly engraved to show what the tournament was and who won it. On a shelf above the bar in our club there are a number of beer mugs. Each one bears a member's name, and only that member can ever drink from it. The mugs are trophies from various special tournaments. And you should see the owners expand their chests and swagger to the bar as they call for their own private mugs! Every time the mug is used, it's a reminder to the trophy-holder, and to all beholders, that he is the champ of some tournament or other. Maybe it's the only trophy he ever won. All the better. He prizes it the more.

Remember that club tournaments are run to get a lot of people out on the courts—to mix them with other members they don't know—to give everyone some good exercise and some fun. Club tournaments are *not* run (with the exception of the annual championship tourney) to find out who is the best player in the club. If you can get lots of tournament trophies scattered through the club membership—on all levels, not just among the top layer of players—then you can consider that your tournament committee is doing a good job.

Planning and Politeness Pay

A tournament won't run by itself. Your committee has got to start the wheels turning, and keep them turning. It isn't enough just to post a notice on the bulletin board, as some clubs do, announcing "A tournament will be held beginning on June 10. All players wishing to enter sign up at the office."

Get some artistic member to make up some big posters, with bright color and heavy lettering, to announce the tourney. Then plant the posters all over the club—in the locker rooms, on the courts, at the bar, in the lobby and the dining room. Follow this up by buttonholing every member you know, to make sure he enters.

Lay your plans carefully. Schedule matches for a day and hour that you're sure is agreeable to both players. Then make sure that each gets a post card a couple of days before the match reminding him of it. Even this isn't enough. Make a point of telephoning each player, on the evening before his match, to tell him once more that he's scheduled to play and get his assurance that he'll be there.

In spite of all these precautions, some players aren't going to show up at the appointed hour. Should you rule the match a default? Not on your life!

This isn't Seabright or Wimbledon. You're not dealing with full-time tennis players. These are people with busy and complicated lives. Tennis is only one of their interests. If you arbitrarily oust a man from a club tournament, you disappoint his opponent and you run a risk of killing his own interest in this and future tournaments. Be nice to your entrants. Be suave, diplomatic, and polite. If a man is late for his match, telephone him to find out why. If he's merely delayed temporarily, cajole his opponent into waiting. If he can't make it that day, try to reschedule the match for another day. Remember, the big idea is to get as many players onto those courts as possible—not to ram the schedule through like a railroad timetable.

In every club tournament there are always one or two players who want to change the draw. They argue that you shouldn't have thrown them in against the opponent you did, that they'd much rather play someone else. Be polite to these characters, even though they get in your hair. Explain to them that the draw was made by a representative group of players who knew everyone's ability. (This is where your tournament committee gets off the hook, if you've called in an advisory panel of players to help you make the seedings or the handicaps or the draw. But if your tournament committee has taken all this power unto itself, then you're in for a few assorted brickbats and dead cats, and you'll just have to stand up there and take them.)

Sometimes you ought to make concessions to the complainers who want to change opponents, even though it fouls up your beautifully laid plans. When a couple of dubs ask to be allowed to play each other in the first round, instead of squaring off against big shots who are sure to knock them out of the tournament immediately, you'll be wise to listen. If you can rearrange your draw to give those two unfortunates the thrill of having one good hammer-and-tongs battle before they're eliminated from the tournament, do it.

Just keep in mind this one principle, and you won't go far wrong: aim to make a club tournament provide as much fun as possible for as many people as possible. If you act on that principle, you'll be the best-liked tournament committeeman your club has ever had.

27 / On Your Way!

It Works

My wife Jerry plays a little tennis. Just a little. She says she gets too tired to play more than a set or two. And I suppose she has a right to feel tired because she's a pretty tiny kid. But anyhow, Jerry got to reading the manuscript of one of the earlier chapters of this book not long ago. She put it down with a thoughtful look and went out on the club courts for a friendly game with the first girl she could corral.

A while later she came bursting into my room. "Bob, it works, it works!" she screamed. "It's wonderful! Why didn't you tell me this long ago?"

"Relax, honey," I yawned. "Stop babbling and tell me what works."

"Why, your book!"

"I know, darling. It ought to work. I spent years figuring out what to put in that book."

She shot me a disgusted look. "Then you've been holding out on me all these years. You never told me half the things you're telling the whole world in that book."

"Such as?"

"Such as how to keep from getting tired on the tennis court. I tried out all those things you put in the book—about walking slowly, and taking time between serves, and breathing, and relaxing, and all the rest of it. Bob, it was heavenly! I played almost twice as long as I usually do, and I still don't feel a bit tired. Why didn't you tell me long ago?"

Well, the argument continued far into the night because I maintained I'd told her time and time again—but I won't bore you with further details. The point is that people seem to get more good out of reading an idea in a book than they do from hearing it face to face. Many other people have had an advance peek at various chapters and tell me the same thing. This is a surprise to me, but it's a good omen for the success of this book.

Somehow, by putting all my teaching down in black and white, item by item, I've apparently been able to give tennis players something that produces immediate results when they try it. I've had my share of success in coaching people personally, but until now I haven't been sure that the same coaching would percolate through the pages of a book, when I wasn't present to demonstrate to a pupil and guide his arm through the right motions.

I hope you'll keep coming back to this book again and again. You can't remember everything in it after just one reading, or even two. Each time you dip into it, you'll find something you haven't yet started putting into practice. Concentrate on one skill at a time, keep thinking about it all through a session or two on the courts, and you'll get it thoroughly. Then you can go on to the next skill and master it, too. There are at least five years of steady improvement ahead of you, if you use this book as it's meant to be used, a chapter at a time.

I think you'll have fun with it. There's a great thrill in beating someone who'd always wiped the court with you in the past—and that's the kind of thrill I believe you can get. Just by stepping your game up one or two notches, just by applying one or two principles of sophisticated tennis, you'll find yourself moving ahead of players who used to beat you regularly.

But winning isn't the big idea of this book. The big idea is to do yourself good through playing tennis. You don't do yourself any particular good by winning. But you can do yourself a world of good by using tennis as a means to health and a mental tonic. If you come off the court feeling pleasantly relaxed instead of exhausted, in high good humor instead of mad at the world, then tennis will be a wonderful medicine for you.

So keep that big idea always in mind as you use this book That's the way to get the most from tennis. Here's hoping you find that the book helps you to play winning tennis incidentally, but happy tennis primarily!

Index